T0151930

A
DYBBUK

A
DYBBUK

Adapted by

Tony Kushner

Translated from S. Ansky by Joachim Neugroschel

Afterword by Harold Bloom

AND

THE
DYBBUK MELODY
And Other Themes and Variations

Translated by Joachim Neugroschel

THEATRE COMMUNICATIONS GROUP

The adaptation of *A Dybbuk or Between Two Worlds*
is copyright © 1998 by Tony Kushner
The Dybbuk Melody and Other Themes and Variations
translations are copyright © 1998 by Joachim Neugroschel
Afterword is copyright © 1998 by Harold Bloom

A Dybbuk and Other Tales of the Supernatural is published by
Theatre Communications Group, Inc., 355 Lexington Ave.,
New York, NY 10017–0217.

All rights reserved. Except for brief passages quoted in newspaper, magazine,
radio or television reviews, no part of this book may be reproduced in any
form or by any means, electronic or mechanical, including photocopying or
recording, or by an information storage and retrieval system, without permission in writing from the publisher.

Regarding performance: Professionals and amateurs are hereby warned that
this material, being fully protected under the Copyright Laws of the United
States of America and all other countries of the Berne and Universal Copyright
Conventions, is subject to a royalty. All rights including, but not limited to, pro-
fessional, amateur, recording, motion picture, recitation, lecturing, public reading, radio and television broadcasting, and the rights of translation into foreign
languages are expressly reserved. Particular emphasis is placed on the question
of readings and all uses of this book by educational institutions, permission for
which must be secured from the author's representative: The Joyce Ketay
Agency, 1501 Broadway, New York, NY 10036, (212) 354-6825.

Kushner, Tony.
A dybbuk and other tales of the supernatural / translated and adapted from
S. Ansky and others : by Tony Kushner and Joachim Neugroschel.
ISBN 1–55936–1146–8 (alk. paper).
ISBN 1–55936–137–9 (pbk. : alk. paper)
1. Yiddish literature—Translations into English. 2. Fantastic fiction,
Yiddish—Translations into English. I. An-Ski, S., 1863–1920. Dibek.
English. II. Neugroschel, Joachim. III. Title.
PJ5191.E1K87 1997   97–48351
839'.108–dc21   CIP

Cover picture copyright © 1998 by Maurice Sendak
Cover design by Cynthia Krupat
Text design and composition by Lisa Govan

First Edition, March 1998
Third Printing, January 2016

Contents

A DYBBUK OR BETWEEN TWO WORLDS
Adaptation by Tony Kushner   1

AFTERWORD
by Harold Bloom   109

THE DYBBUK MELODY AND
OTHER THEMES AND VARIATIONS
Translations by Joachim Neugroschel   113

    Introduction   115

    The Dybbuk Melody   117

    A Human Life   120

    The Creation Melody   125

    The Ten Signs of the Messiah   127

    The Shepherd's Melody   144

    Gehenna   146

    The Gallows Melody   158

    God on Trial   160

    Keeping Watch   169

Contents

The Girls' Melody 183

Joy 185

The Egyptian Passover 190

The Rabbi's Melody
or A Melody That Unlocks
the Secrets of the Torah 196

A DYBBUK

or Between Two Worlds

A Dramatic Legend in Four Acts

Adaptation by
Tony Kushner

Written by
S. Ansky

Translated from Yiddish by
Joachim Neugroschel

THIS ADAPTATION IS FOR MARK LAMOS,

WITH LOVE AND GRATITUDE;

AND FOR THE MEMORY OF

BETTY OSBORNE

A Dybbuk or Between Two Worlds received its world premiere in February 1995 at Hartford Stage Company, Hartford, CT, (Mark Lamos, Artistic Director; Stephen J. Albert, Managing Director). The set was designed by John Conklin, lights by Pat Collins, costumes by Jess Goldstein, sound by David Budries and original music was composed by The Klezmatics. Mark Lamos directed the following cast:

CHONEN	Michael Hayden
THE THREE BATLONIM	Daniel Zelman, Richard Topol, Eddie Castrodad
THE MESSENGER	Michael Stuhlbarg
MAYER	David Little
AN OLD WOMAN	Nancy Franklin
HENECH	Gordon MacDonald
FRADDE	Judith Roberts
LEAH	Julie Dretzin
GITL	Elizabeth Sastre
SENDER	Robert LuPone
THE WEDDING GUEST	Herman Petras
A VERY OLD POOR WOMAN	Nancy Franklin
BESSYE	Alison Russo
NACHMAN	Yusef Bulos
RABBI MENDL	Gordon MacDonald
MENASHE	Richard Topol
RABBI AZRIEL	Sam Gray
MICHL	Herman Petras
THE SCRIBE	Mark Feuerstein
RABBI SHIMSHIN	Yusef Bulos
THE RABBINICAL JUDGES	Gordon MacDonald, H. A. Shemonsky

The play was produced in November 1997 at New York City's Joseph Papp Public Theater/New York Shakespeare Festival (George C. Wolfe, Producer; Rosemarie Tichler, Artistic Producer; Anne F. Zimmerman, Managing Director). The set was designed by Mark Wendland, lights by Mimi Jordan Sherin, costumes by Elizabeth Hope Clancy, sound by Tom Morse and original music was composed by The Klezmatics. Brian Kulick directed the following cast:

CHONEN	Michael Stuhlbarg
THE THREE BATLONIM	David Lipman,
	Stuart Zagnit,
	Ümit Çelebi
THE MESSENGER	Ed Shea
MAYER	Joshua Mostel
AN OLD WOMAN	Joan Copeland
HENECH	Stephen Kunken
FRADDE	Lola Pashalinski
LEAH	Marin Hinkle
GITL	Eve Michelson
SENDER	Robert Dorfman
BEGGAR	Christopher McCann
A POOR WOMAN WITH A BABY	Nina Goldman
A POOR WOMAN	Joyce Chittick
A VERY OLD POOR WOMAN	Marcell Rosenblatt
GHOST OF LEAH'S MOTHER	Nina Goldman
HOLY BRIDE	Joyce Chittick
HOLY BRIDEGROOM	Daniel Wright
BESSYE	Joyce Chittick
NACHMAN	Stuart Zagnit
RABBI MENDL	Bernie Passeltiner

MENASHE	Hillel Meltzer
MRS. NACHMAN	Joan Copeland
PASSENGERS	David Lipman,
	Stuart Zagnit,
	Ümit Çelebi
RABBI AZRIEL	Ron Leibman
MICHL	Bernie Passeltiner
THE SCRIBE	Hillel Meltzer
RABBI SHIMSHIN	Christopher McCann
CHASIDS	Stephen Kunken,
	Ümit Çelebi,
	Stuart Zagnit
THE RABBINICAL JUDGES	Joshua Mostel,
	David Lipman

CAST

CHONEN, a former yeshiva student, now a rabbi, who, having wandered, has returned to Brinnitz

THE THREE BATLONIM, or idlers, who are employed by the community to hang out at the synagogue to fill out a minyan when necessary

THE MESSENGER

MAYER, the shammes (beadle) of the Brinnitz synagogue

OLD WOMAN, named Channa-Esther, whose daughter is dying

HENECH, a yeshiva student, a friend of Chonen

FRADDE, Leah's old nurse

LEAH, the daughter of Sender of Brinnitz

GITL, Leah's friend

SIX OR SEVEN YESHIVA STUDENTS, studying late in the Brinnitz synagogue

SENDER OF BRINNITZ, a wealthy man, follower of Rabbi Azriel of Miropol

TWO OR THREE WEALTHY FRIENDS OF SENDER

FOUR BEGGARS

A POOR WOMAN WITH A BABY

A LAME WOMAN

A VERY HOMELY MAN

A VERY OLD POOR WOMAN

BESSYE, Leah's friend

NACHMAN, father of the bridegroom

RABBI MENDL, teacher of the bridegroom

MENASHE, the bridegroom

MRS. NACHMAN, MENASHE'S AUNTS and UNCLES and COUSINS

A TALL PALE WOMAN

THREE PASSENGERS

RABBI AZRIEL OF MIROPOL, a great Chasidic rabbi, a tzaddik

MICHL, the gabbe (manager) of Rabbi Azriel

THE SCRIBE, Azriel's court's recording secretary

RABBI SHIMSHIN, the Chief Rabbi of Miropol

THREE CHASIDS, all followers of Rabbi Azriel of Miropol

TWO RABBINICAL JUDGES

The first and second acts take place in Brinnitz,
the third and fourth acts take place in Miropol,
in Poland, at the end of the nineteenth century.

Act One

SCENE 1

Before the curtain, in near darkness, Chonen is washing himself in a ritual bath. He chants:

CHONEN

Why did the soul,
Oh tell me this,
Tumble from Heaven
To the Great Abyss?
The most profound descents contain
Ascensions to the heights again . . .

(Darkness engulfs the scene.)

SCENE 2

The curtain rises slowly.
A small wooden synagogue; its walls blackened with great age and candlesmoke. The roof is held up by two wooden columns. At the center of the ceiling, above the sloping bimah (the platform from which the Torah is read), an old brass lamp, with a single light, is hanging. The bimah is covered with a dark tablecloth. On the rear wall, several small windows with wooden grillwork indicate the womens' gallery. A long table with a wooden bench; on the table are heaps of books, sacred texts, scrolls. Among the books are a few clay candleholders in which tallow candles are burning. To one side of the table, in the rear wall also, is the small door to the rabbi's private study. In a corner near the door is a bookcase containing very old sacred books. In the center of the right-hand wall is the Holy Ark, in which the Torah scrolls are kept. To the left of the Ark is the cantor's rough wooden lectern, upon which a large yahrzeit (memorial) candle is burning, guttering, dripping wax. On either side of the Holy Ark is a window, dark now, it's late at night. There are benches and bookcases along the length of the rest of the wall. On the left-hand wall there is a large tile stove, next to which is another bench and a table, laden with holy books; next to this is a ritual washstand, behind which is a towel hanging from an iron towel ring. Near the washstand is the wide door that leads to the street. Near the door there is a chest; above the chest there is a ner-tomid (an eternal light in a glass-chimneyed hanging lamp).
Henech is sitting on a bench near the cantor's stand, studying a holy book. Five or six younger yeshiva students are sprawled on the bench at the rear wall, drowsing through texts while softly humming a dreamy Talmudic melody. Mayer, the beadle, is laying out cloth sacks containing prayer shawls and phylacteries.

The three Batlonim (idlers), heads in the clouds, books face-down on their laps, are sitting at the left-wall table, schmoozing and klatching. The Messenger is lying on the bench near the stove, his head resting on his traveler's pack. In the corner, Chonen stands by the case full of ancient texts, silent and remote, thinking, praying to himself.

Deep evening has settled into the synagogue, deepening its shadowy corners, creating a mysterious, mystical atmosphere.

FIRST BATLON
Before the soul can be inspired,
Holiness is first attired
In glory which the world can see,
In Visible Epiphany!

SECOND BATLON
The Levites, in the days of Old,
Dressed themselves in Cloth of Gold!

FIRST BATLON
And even now, bejeweled, impearled,
Tzaddikim walk the lower world!

SECOND BATLON
Rabbi Dovid of Talna sat on a big chair made all of gold. Rabbi Yisroel of Rizhin of blessed memory went about in a gold-curtained carriage pulled by six gray horses.

THIRD BATLON
Rabbi Shmuel of Kaminka always wore gold slippers. And that's not apocryphal: I personally saw them. Gold slippers!

THE MESSENGER
(Sitting up on the bench, in a quiet, faraway voice) Rabbi Zusye of Anapol lived and died in poverty. His clothes were peasants' rags and he begged in the streets. But he was as holy as anyone who's lived.

(Little pause. The Batlonim look at the recumbent stranger, who has not risen from his bench.)

FIRST BATLON

Pardon me, but who asked you to contribute?

THE MESSENGER

I was intrigued. I have some experience of the wide world, and I have rarely seen that Holiness attires itself in expensive clothes.

FIRST BATLON

Of course! But gold is symbolic!

THIRD BATLON

A metaphor! For holiness! Gold in and of itself is valueless, but . . .

SECOND BATLON

Oh don't jump to that conclusion so hastily! Poor Jews always equate poverty and virtue, and that's why we stay poor! We're suspicious of gold. And why? Because when we dwelt in the Holy Land we were surrounded by mighty nations of great wealth and sensuality. As the Torah and the Prophets tell us: the Assyrians had stone cities and brazen armies, the Babylonians their fragrant gardens, the Phoenicians their great ports and marketplaces, and the golden palaces of Pharaoh in Mitzrayim. So in opposition to these cruel and sensual peoples we developed a violent loathing for the splendor of surfaces. To this day!

FIRST BATLON

Interesting point. Did the Almighty not give us the sun? And moon- and candlelight? And do these bright and flickering lights not radiate from the Holy fire, and doesn't gold magnify and worship the light? Is gold not therefore Holy? It comes from the Almighty! I think it's an interesting point.

THIRD BATLON

It's tricky and dangerous. I fear all such twisty argumentation! This is a shul! A holy place! Think only of holiness here, talk of gold leads to talk of desire which leads to talk of . . . of *women* and talk of women . . . Well, men are from earth and women are from bone, as it's written.

FIRST BATLON

I agree, let's not talk about such things, not here, not at night, we'll inadvertently summon The Evil One. *(He spits)*

SECOND BATLON

(Spitting, then) The Devil can't enter a Holy place, not even if you invoke Him! There's nothing in the Holy books, no chants or incantations, not even in the Kabbalah for calling forth Satan. *(He spits)*

THE MESSENGER

Actually there is a way.

(Chonen looks up and turns toward the Messenger, who directs the following at him:)

THE MESSENGER

Whisper the Unutterable Name of God, once, which is a terrible sin, and then twice. It is after this act of defiance that the Angel of Light was hurled from Paradise into abysmal eternal night. And he waits in night there to answer the call of his acolytes.

THIRD BATLON

It's terribly dangerous to even think of speaking that Name.

THE MESSENGER

For Jews there is always danger everywhere. But the vessel will burst only if the spark within lusts too hotly for the flame without.

FIRST BATLON

In the shtetl of my birth there's a miracle-working rabbi who can make candles ignite by whispering the Holy Name, and if he whispers it again they all go out. He can see for hundreds of miles around, he knows everything that's happening, he drums his fingers on stone walls and wine dribbles from the cracks. He told me he'd made a golem, back when the persecutions grew too frequent and too fierce; he told me how he'd made the dead rise, he could fly invisible through the air and devils danced at his behest. He even conjured Satan. *(He spits)* My rabbi is the one who told me: "Within and within, turn your eyes inwards . . ."

CHONEN

(In a voice like the Messenger's, a faraway voice) Where can I find him?

FIRST BATLON

Who?

CHONEN

This rabbi who works miracles.

FIRST BATLON

He's . . . In his house, I imagine, in my shtetl, if he's still amongst the living.

CHONEN

Is it far?

FIRST BATLON

My shtetl? In deepest Polisia, leagues away. It would take a month at least to walk there.

CHONEN

What's his name?

FIRST BATLON

Why, Reb Chonen? You want to visit him?

(Chonen stares at the Batlonim, and then at the Messenger, silent.)

FIRST BATLON

The shtetl's called Krasne. The rabbi's name is Elchonen.

CHONEN

Thank you.

(He starts to turn back to his corner, but stops and looks at the First Batlon.)

El-Chonen. The God of Chonen. Perhaps I should visit him.

(Chonen goes back to his corner.)

THE MESSENGER

(To the First Batlon) Who is he?

FIRST BATLON

A yeshiva student.

(Mayer closes the gate in front of the bimah and comes over to the table.)

SECOND BATLON

Some sort of genius, they say. A prodigious memory.

THIRD BATLON

He's swallowed over five hundred pages of the Talmud, every letter, every word. The boy's got a magical mind.

THE MESSENGER

Where's he from?

MAYER

A Litvak, I think. He studied here, best of the whole yeshiva, he was elevated to the rabbinate, easy, but then for a whole year following his ordination, he disappeared! Some said he was atoning for sins, others that he wandered in exile; and then, just recently, he came back! But he's not the same boy who left. For one thing, he's a million miles away, all the time, deep inside his thoughts. He doesn't eat anything, except on Shabbes, and then not so much as would satisfy a mouse. And day and night he's in the ritual baths, washing; he's just come from there. *(Lowering his voice)* He's reading the Kabbalah . . .

SECOND BATLON
(Also softly) The whole town's talking. People have asked him for charms. He refuses.

THIRD BATLON
He might be a Holy man, perhaps one of the Just. It's dangerous to nose about in such things.

SECOND BATLON
And besides *(He yawns)* it's very late. Bedtime. *(To the First Batlon)* Pity your wondrous rabbi isn't here to drum his fingers, draw a little brandy from the walls to warm our dreams.

FIRST BATLON
Or maybe he could pull a buckwheat cookie from his hat! I haven't eaten all day, only one biscuit after prayers.

MAYER
Tell your stomach, "Just a little longer, stomach," and tell your throat the same—it'll be wet before long, I'll bet.

FIRST BATLON
Do tell.

MAYER
Sender is off visiting a prospective bridegroom for his daughter!

FIRST BATLON
So?

MAYER

So? So if they sign a marriage contract, he'll treat us all to drinks and dinner!

SECOND BATLON

And if Moshiach comes tonight, I won't have to work in the morning.

THIRD BATLON

You don't work anyway.

FIRST BATLON

Sender's already been to see—what is it now?—three bridegrooms, and three times no contract. The first time it was the boy that was wrong, the second time it was the family, and what was the matter with the third one?

THIRD BATLON

The dowry.

FIRST BATLON

Right! Sender deliberately offered too little. It's a sin to bargain in bad faith.

MAYER

Sender can afford to pick and choose, he's rich from a rich family, his daughter is beautiful—Heaven shine upon her.

THIRD BATLON

Sender is a wonderful man, a real Chasid, a Rabbi-of-Miropol Chasid, and those Miropol Chasids, their faith is amazing.

FIRST BATLON

No one could argue that he's a devout Chasid, he should try nevertheless a different approach to finding his daughter a husband, is all I'm saying.

THIRD BATLON

For instance?

FIRST BATLON

Like in my father's time, even rich from a rich family, when a man sought a suitor for his daughter, he would bring the Grand Rebbe of some Great Yeshiva a nice gift and say, "Which is the best student?" Not who is the richest student, but the smartest, the most wise. Maybe Sender should be doing that.

THE MESSENGER

His daughter's bridegroom might be right here.

THIRD BATLON

Here?

(The Messenger shrugs.)

THIRD BATLON

Marriages are made when the bride and the groom belong to each other. They can't be arranged, not really.

(The outside door bursts open and an Old Woman enters.)

OLD WOMAN

Out of my way, everyone.

MAYER

Woman, go away, you're not permitted here!

OLD WOMAN

I must come in! I want to shove my head in the Ark!

MAYER

God forbid!

OLD WOMAN

I want to shriek at the Torahs. I want to douse the flickering little ner-tomid light with my tears. The King of the Universe is taking my child! MY DAUGHTER IS DYING!

(The students and Batlonim hiss and shush her.)

THIRD BATLON

You see, this is why women aren't permitted in the . . .

OLD WOMAN

God of Abraham, Isaac and Jacob, please don't take my daughter from this world, look at how young she is! Matriarchs, run up to the throne of the Lord of Creation, shout your grief as loudly as I shout mine, tell Him who made you, Matriarchs, on my daughter's behalf, tell Him you will pull the Universe down, stone by stone, unless He promises He'll restore my daughter completely to life!

MAYER

(Crossing to her) Channa-Esther, quiet please, this shrilling in shul is a sin. Maybe I should find ten men for a minyan, we could chant the psalms?

OLD WOMAN

Do it, do it now, why do you need to ask? She's losing her battle with the butcher-angel, praised be He, hurry!

MAYER

Immediately, but we have to give the men something for their trouble. They're poor.

OLD WOMAN

(Rummaging in her pocket) Here, a ruble. Just make sure they say every psalm.

MAYER

A ruble is just a kopek or two per man, Channa-Esther, perhaps...

(The Old Woman heads for the door.)

OLD WOMAN

I can't stand here talking to you, I have to visit every synagogue in Brinnitz! MY DAUGHTER IS DYING!

(She leaves in a hurry.)

THE MESSENGER

Earlier today, another woman was here. She too wanted to put her head in the Ark. Her daughter was in labor, and had been for two days, in terrible pain. She wanted the Almighty to let her daughter give birth. One daughter wrestles with death, the other with birth.

THIRD BATLON

So?

THE MESSENGER

Perhaps the soul of the dying daughter is intended for the body of the baby who won't be born. Who would be born, without a soul? Who wants to die, and relinquish the soul? If this sick daughter dies, the laboring daughter will deliver her child. If the sick daughter recovers, the baby will be born dead.

THIRD BATLON

The world is full of mysteries, and people never see them.

FIRST BATLON

(To the drowsing yeshiva students) Wake up! Come to the rabbi's study, we have psalms to chant for the sake of an ailing mother.

MAYER

Everyone who joins in gets a drink of kvass and a buckwheat cake.

(The students, the Batlonim and Mayer go into the study. Soon a mournful recitation of the First Psalm, "Blessed be the man who walks not in the counsel of the ungodly . . ." is heard from within. The Messenger and Chonen are left behind. The Messenger watches Chonen.)

THE MESSENGER

Chonen?

(Chonen turns. He sees that the Ark is open.)

CHONEN

Who opened the Ark? It's nearly midnight . . .

THE MESSENGER

A grieving woman opened it.

CHONEN

A young woman, or old?

THE MESSENGER

Not young.

CHONEN

Not . . . The Torah scrolls are inside like dark men engulfed in shadow, draped in velvet shawls, bent over mysteries. There are nine scrolls here, the number you get when you add up the letters of "Emes," so truth is here, and each of these nine has four wooden spokes, and four times nine is thirty-six, isn't it, which is a number that confronts me everywhere, every day, thirty-six. There's a name. Leah. What number is the letter Lamed?

THE MESSENGER

Thirty.

CHONEN

Exactly. And Aleph is one, and Hey is five. Thirty-six. So it's Leah, obviously, who is waiting for me everywhere, she's hidden in everything, and thrice thirty-six is one hundred and eight, which is the value of Chonen, and three times . . . But also from Leah, Lamed and Hey, one can spell "Not God." Not from God. Leah Not From God.

THE MESSENGER

A terrible thought.

CHONEN

Yes, but I can't stop thinking it, it wants me to think it, it's always there, waiting to be thought, it even gives me a sunless shadow sort of pleasure. Don't tell anyone . . .

THE MESSENGER

I am a messenger, you can trust to my discretion.

CHONEN

You aren't from Brinnitz, but you seem . . .

THE MESSENGER

Familiar, yes, I seem so to most people, but I'm always a stranger. Tell me a tale, Reb Chonen.

CHONEN

There's a man in this town, wealthy and impressive, a great . . . hoarder of precious things, and he has a daughter, and she is . . . I've been back a month and I've seen more than I want to see but I haven't seen her since returning; I fled from here, from her, from dreams I had in which she . . . Wherever I've gone, and I have wandered . . . *very* far, she follows me, in dreams, she begs me to return, and in me a certainty has grown, and I am certain it's from God, that she is *mine*, not his, not her father's nor anyone else's. God wants me to return, to claim her, to say any prayer, chant any spell in any book to save her from her father's . . . from his dealings, but God keeps her from me. He's shut her up inside, one by one I defeat his plans, I . . . I'm *impressed*, these incantations *work*! The Almighty speaks sometimes out of the mouths of salamanders and unclean things, and I'm . . . *astonished*, but nothing, nothing brings her to me, and . . .

(Henech enters.)

HENECH

Chonen?

(Chonen turns, and the Messenger disappears.)

HENECH

Come sit by me. You stand in the corner, or you wander the town, dreaming, fantasizing. You have such a mind for the Law, but you waste your days playing with numbers, adding and multiplying, you're no better than a businessman. Let's read the Holy books together.

CHONEN

What Holy books?

HENECH

(Shocked) The Talmud. The Commentaries.

CHONEN

The Talmud is bleak and cold. The Commentaries are barren. Beneath this earth there's another world just like this one, with farms and forests, oceans, deserts, cities, villages, great storms tossing great ships on the seas, terror in the woods, and cease-less thunder; but in this underworld there's no sky, and no light, only a black ceiling of gravedirt and root-ends, not lightning bolts, no sun. That's the Talmud. Deep and broad and mar-velous enough, but earth above and earth below and you can't ever rise up with the Talmud. The Kabbalah . . . is different.

HENECH

You're lost in the tangled words of that book.

CHONEN

Its thorns have caught my soul up, its branches have hurled me
toward Heaven, between its covers I've had glimpses of inner
rooms, chambers and back alleys in the palaces of God, I have
enfolded my suffering heart in the pages of the Kabbalah and
my heart has burst into flame there, eyes within eyes have
opened wide and seen the edges of the great dark curtain lift.

HENECH

Listen to me, Chonen. We were students together. You frighten
me now, you've flown too far, and I don't trust your means of
ascent. Read the Talmud, it can lift you to God, but in slow
and sure steps, stone by stone. The Talmud guides you along
the true path, and it doesn't let you wander. The Kabbalah is
all twisting, deviating, writhing. Don't rush to get to Paradise.
Remember the four rabbis:

(He begins to intone a Talmudic melody:)

Four rabbis entered Paradise: Azzai, Zoma, Aher, Akiba.
Rabbi ben Azzai looked about and died.
ben Zoma went mad there, returned a mad wraith,
Trampling tender plants, seducing the young,
Aher crossed over to the Other Side.
But Akiba survived it, strong in his faith.

CHONEN

Those rabbis used to scare me, not anymore. Others have followed them to Paradise and come back—the holiest of men,
the Baal Shem Tov did it; not everyone who gets there is
destroyed.

HENECH

But you aren't the Baal Shem Tov.

CHONEN

I don't claim to be. I have my own path.

HENECH

Instruct me, explain to me.

CHONEN

I can't.

HENECH

Please. I want to know. I yearn to see Paradise, the same as you,
I have a soul that seeks the Fire.

(Little pause.)

CHONEN

The tzaddikim walk among us, and these saints have as their
occupation scrubbing sin from human souls, to renew the soul's
perfect original brightness. But evils crowd 'round every doorway. Clean a soul of seventy sins, polish it bright, it will come
back at once even more spotted. Purify a whole generation and
the next generation appears, unrepentant. And each generation grows more stiff-necked, and the tzaddikim grow fewer
and weaker, and to us it seems that evil is withering the world.

HENECH

Then what should we do?

CHONEN

(Quiet and certain) We should not try to banish sin, but to
make sin holy. Like the goldsmith with his delicate ladles, his
small hot flames, his precise and cautious gestures; the way the
farmer carefully, deliberately divides wheat from chaff; this is
how we purify sin, in the crucibles of our souls, we purify sin
and make sin holy.

HENECH

Holy sin is an impossibility.

CHONEN

God made sin.

HENECH

Not true, Chonen, sin is from the Sitra-achra, it belongs to the Other Side.

CHONEN

And who made the Other Side? The Sitra-achra is God's Other Side. Satan is another side of God. And so Satan must be holy.

HENECH

Please, you're confusing me, I can't understand this.

(Henech buries his face in the book he's been reading. Chonen stands over him, bends down to him and whispers:)

CHONEN

Think of the beautiful Song of Songs. What's it doing in the Bible?

HENECH

Please don't speak to me, Chonen.

CHONEN

(Overlapping) It's full of desire, it's dangerous to read, but it's there because, precisely because lust and desire are the most persistent sins, and in the purifying flame of the Holiest of Holies, even lust and desire have a sound like this:

Behold, you are fair, my love, you are fair;
Your eyes are like doves,
You are pleasing and fair,
And our bed is made of soft leaves,
And our roof beam is cedar,
And the walls of our house are of cypress.
I am the rose of Sharon,
A lily of the valleys,
Like a lily among thorns is my love among the daughters.
And my beloved is an apple tree among the trees of the wood,

Under his shadow I delighted to sit,
And his fruit was sweet to my tongue.
He has brought me to the banquet hall, and his banner is love.
Oh refresh me with apples, for I am love-sick . . .

(Leah enters the sanctuary. Chonen instantly stops reciting and stares at her.
Mayer emerges from the rabbi's study, just as, behind Leah, Fradde and Gitl enter. The women hesitate by the door.)

FRADDE

We knocked. Someone was praying and didn't hear us, but we knocked.

MAYER

Sender's daughter! An honor!

LEAH

(Timid) You promised me, Mayer, you'd show me the old curtains for the Ark.

(Leah looks at Chonen, then looks down and doesn't look back.)

FRADDE

You know the ones, Mayer, the old embroidered curtains, Leah promised new ones on the anniversary of her mother's death. She can embroider like they used to, with heavy gold and silver thread, lions and eagles and pomegranates. You can hang the new curtains on the Ark and they'll sparkle like her mother's soul in Paradise.

MAYER

Right away! *(He goes back into the study)*

GITL

(Whispering to Leah) I don't like it here at night, it's grim and frightening.

LEAH

I've never been in a synagogue this late before, except on Simchas Torah, when everyone's dancing and all the candles are lit. It's brooding tonight, mourning over lost lives, it's heartbreaking, it's dark as the bottom of the sea.

FRADDE

Sure it's a sad place at night and I'll tell you why that is. The dead come to pray here at the shul at night, scattering their sorrows on the floor like dead leaves, leaving piles of sorrows all over the place.

GITL

Stop it, Fradde, you know I hate ghost stories.

FRADDE

And you want to know why the walls are wet? Touch them, see if I'm telling stories—they're wet! That's because every morning when the sun rises fresh on the happy world, the Almighty weeps to remember how the Temple was destroyed, and the walls of every synagogue run wet with His tears. That's why the walls are never cleaned—so we remember how dark and bitter it's been. Whitewash those walls, and stones will fall on your head and kill you.

LEAH

From the outside, or from the balcony, or when it's all lit up, you can't tell how old it is. But it's very very old.

FRADDE

Oh my darling, it's inconceivably old. They say it wasn't built, just found buried underground, the whole building. And even though the village has been burned to the ground again and again, so many times, the synagogue never burns. Once they set the roof afire, but doves came flying, hundreds of doves, from out of the synagogue roof, clasping the flames in their wings, bearing the fire up away from the shul, and so it was saved.

LEAH

I'd like to stay here all night if I could, and kneel by the walls and ask them their secrets, why they weep and for whom, every person, name by name, ask them to tell me what they dream at night. Their silence draws me.

(Mayer returns with the curtains.)

MAYER

Handle them carefully, they're hundreds of years old, they were stitched by a rebbetzin who lived and died among the Jews of Spain, before the exile from there began.

(As they examine the curtains:)

GITL

Leah, there's a boy over there, staring . . .

LEAH

He's from the yeshiva. Chonen.

GITL

You know him?

FRADDE

Look at this velvet. Sure it's disintegrating but how deep the plush is, it's so heavy.

LEAH

Sometimes he came to our house for meals.

GITL

He's afraid of you. He wants to come closer but he can't.

LEAH

He looks pale and thin and unhappy. Do you think he's been ill?

GITL

Oh I don't think he's unhappy. Look at his eyes.

LEAH

They're always like that, incredible eyes, and when he talked to me he spoke with short, tight breaths. And that's how I talked to him.

GITL

No wonder you made Fradde bring us here, it wasn't the curtains.

LEAH

It's wrong to talk and he's a stranger.

FRADDE

Mayer, we have to go now and we can't visit God without kissing the Torahs.

MAYER

Naturally, just don't tell the rabbi, let me get one.

(Mayer goes to the Ark, followed by Gitl and Fradde. Leah lags behind, and looks at Chonen. A little pause, then:)

LEAH

Good evening, Chonen. You've come back from your travels.

CHONEN

(Breathless) Yes. I've . . . returned.

(They look at each other.)

LEAH

You've returned . . .

FRADDE

Leah, come and kiss the Torah!

(Leah goes to Mayer, who's holding the Torah. She kneels, embraces it, and kisses it passionately for a long time.)

FRADDE

That's enough, that's enough, you kiss the Torah quickly, it's made of fire, black and white fire and it'll burn you if you linger. We should get home before your father finds out. *(Nodding goodnight)* Mayer.

(The women leave. Mayer returns the scroll to the Ark and shuts the Ark doors, and then follows the women out.)

CHONEN

(A pause, then)

... For I am lovesick ...
The winter is past, the rain is over and gone,
The time of singing is come,
And the voice of the turtle is heard in our land ...
Until the days breathe, and the shadows flee away ...

HENECH

Stop reciting, Chonen.

(Henech strokes Chonen's hair, pulling one of his payes.)

HENECH

Your hair's wet again. You've been to the ritual baths.

CHONEN

Yes.

HENECH

While you're cleansing your body do you chant spells? Is this what's prescribed in the Book of Raziel the Angel?

(Silence, Chonen doesn't respond.)

HENECH

I'd be afraid.

(Little pause.)

You can't live without eating and you never eat now, only on Shabbes and that's not enough.

CHONEN

I want to stop eating on Shabbes. I've grown to hate the smell of food.

HENECH

What in the name of the Almighty are you doing to yourself?

CHONEN

I've seen . . . A diamond, perfect, a perfect thing, absolute, hard and . . . I want to hold her, and cry, until my tears melt the diamond and then . . . I'll drink her in, and then . . . see . . . something, maybe . . . sunlight striking the domes of the Temple, not the ruined First nor the burnt Second Temple but the Third Temple, the one the future waits to build, I want to see such beauty . . .
(He pauses and sways a little) I am a little weakened by . . . the studies, but . . . There's a way to make gold, did you know that? Two barrels of gold, by shaping letters in clay, and I need to learn this, to make gold coins for the man whose only love is counting.

HENECH

You can't do work like that through the Holy One.

CHONEN

Then through some Other way.

HENECH

I'm afraid of you, Chonen. Standing beside you, the things you say.

(Henech leaves the sanctuary. Chonen stands alone, motionless.
The Batlonim emerge from the rabbi's room.)

FIRST BATLON

Eighteen psalms is psalms enough.

SECOND BATLON

Eighteen after all symbolizes life, and for a few kopeks I'm not
going to do all one hundred and fifty psalms.

THIRD BATLON

We should have stayed with the others, we broke the minyan.

SECOND BATLON

They'll be here all night.

(Mayer comes in from the outside.)

MAYER

Well you were right. I just met Borech the tailor coming home
from Klimovke, and he traveled with a man from there who
knew the parents of this latest prospect for Sender's daughter,
and this man told Borech that Sender and the bridegroom's
parents hadn't been able to settle terms, Sender wanting the
bridegroom's family to house the couple for ten years, they
countered with five years, Sender says it's not enough and so
another wedding scratched. Number four!

CHONEN

(Sitting heavily on a bench, to himself) I win again.

THIRD BATLON

Four in a row. A real shame.

THE MESSENGER

(To the Third Batlon) You said so yourself: the Almighty, not
fathers, makes marriages.

THIRD BATLON

Did I say that?

THE MESSENGER

You did.

(The Messenger stands up, lights his lantern and picks up his pack.)

THE MESSENGER

Good night everyone. I've stayed longer than I should.

THIRD BATLON

Don't go, let's talk some more.

THE MESSENGER

I'm a messenger, I work for wealthy and powerful clients, they use me to deliver important messages and convey valuable possessions back and forth. My time is not my own.

MAYER

Stay till dawn at least.

THE MESSENGER

I can't; it takes from midnight to morning to get where I'm going.

THIRD BATLON

That's how long a prayer takes to reach the Throne of Heaven!

THE MESSENGER

I'll be expected at dawn.

(The rest of the minyan emerges from the study.)

A YESHIVA STUDENT

Finished.

THIRD BATLON

That was fast.

SECOND BATLON

Mazel tov.

FIRST BATLON

God grant the poor woman a complete recovery. Let's pool our rubles for some liquor; the night's gotten chilly, my back is stiff.

MAYER

In the house of God you need only ask.

(Mayer produces a bottle of kvass.
Suddenly the front door is flung open and Sender enters, his hat pushed back, his coat unbuttoned, grinning from ear to ear. Three or four other men, well dressed, follow him.)

MAYER

Reb Sender! Welcome!

SENDER

I was headed home but I stopped by to check up on you.

(Sender takes the bottle from Mayer, looks at the label.)

SENDER

I knew I'd find you with your noses deep in books. Pious Chasids every one.

MAYER

Your daughter was here! Moments ago!

SENDER

Leah? Why was she . . .

MAYER

With a bevy of women! Scrutinizing needlework!

FIRST BATLON
We've been overrun with women tonight.

THIRD BATLON
Drink with us, Reb Sender.

SENDER
Oh but absolutely, only we won't need this potato vodka, I'm buying and it'll be real champagne! Congratulate me! I have signed the contract for my daughter's marriage!

EVERYONE
Mazel tov! Mazel tov!

(While everyone moves to shake Sender's hand, Chonen stands and retreats to his corner.)

MAYER
The tailor said he'd heard you couldn't arrive at satisfactory terms with the boy's father.

THIRD BATLON
To be honest, our hearts were broken.

SENDER
The tailor didn't hear wrong, but I know how to negotiate, and the boy's father knows how to bend, and so Leah will soon be married!

THE MESSENGER
Chonen, you should leave this corner, join the others.

CHONEN
(To the Messenger) No, this is wrong, it's not what's supposed to be, I've worked so hard, fasted and cleansed myself, I said the terrible Angel's prayers!
(Shouts to heaven) I was promised! I've taken steps down road-ways no one's ever walked before, to find her again and . . . and I've been weakened by all these struggles, I can't journey

again, I have nowhere else to look, it's . . . I can pronounce the Name—twice. As you said. I can call on God's other angels, the fallen ones, they'll assist me. You are their messenger, this message you brought was intended for me.

THE MESSENGER
I'm only resting here, Chonen. What must be will be.

(Chonen pulls the Messenger close, and whispers the Name in his ear. The Messenger grimaces in pain. Chonen whispers the Name again, and again the Messenger grimaces.)

CHONEN
I've finally won, I had to win, she is light and I am flame and wherever she is I will be rekindled . . .

(Chonen falls to the floor.)

THE MESSENGER
(Looking at his lantern) The candle's guttered out. I'll light a new one.

(All the lights in the synagogue die out.)

SENDER
Mayer! What's wrong with the candles? Lights!

THE MESSENGER
Reb Sender?

SENDER
Who is that? What happened to the candles?

THE MESSENGER
You've made a deal with someone?

SENDER
Yes, I . . . MAYER! Candles!

THE MESSENGER

At times it happens that fathers make deals and then later break their promises. And it all winds up in Rabbinical Court.

(Mayer lights a candle.)

THE MESSENGER

So be very careful, Reb Sender.

(Sender goes over to Mayer.)

SENDER

Who's that stranger?

MAYER

Just a messenger, from elsewhere . . .

SENDER

Tell him to leave me in peace. Osher! Run to my house and tell the servants to get a midnight feast ready, like Belshazzar!

(One of the students rushes out.)

SENDER

Let's go to my house, everyone. We'll tell stories along the way, of our Rabbi of Miropol—suddenly I'm all nerves, I don't know why! Who knows a story for the journey?

THE MESSENGER

I do.

SENDER

Perhaps someone else can . . .

THE MESSENGER

The Rabbi of Miropol was visited by a very rich Chasid, who was zealous in some respects but also tight-fisted, a miser. The rabbi took the miser's hand and brought him to a window.

"Have a look!" said the rabbi. The miser looked. The rabbi asked, "Well?" The miser said, "I see people on the street." Then the rabbi took his hand again and brought the miser to the hallway mirror. Again the rabbi asked, "Well?" Of course the miser said, "I see myself, Rabbi." The rabbi said, "And do you understand?" Of course the miser didn't. The rabbi said, "The window's made of glass, and so is the mirror. But the mirror has a thin silver coating. All it takes is a silver coat, and suddenly you can't see other people, only yourself."

SENDER

I think you're mocking me.

THIRD BATLON

I liked the story, the rabbi's gentleness is always impressive.

SECOND BATLON

Sing something!

FIRST BATLON

I know a song by the Maggid of Koznitz, who was always infirm but very Holy: it was said in his life he learned this song from the angels, but after his death his disciples informed us: the angels learned it from the Maggid of Koznitz, in fact, these angels who sang were born from his goodness.

(The First Batlon begins to sing a beautiful Chasidic melody; the others join in; the tempo increases.)

SENDER

Let's dance a rikudl! We are Chasids, after all, it's a shame on my honor if I announce my daughter's engagement, and no one joins me in a dance. Let us dance because the Almighty overcomes obstacles and small scrupling and insists on joy! Please, please, everyone join in!

(They form a circle and begin to dance.)

SECOND BATLON

Where's Henech, and Chonen?

SENDER

Chonen! Yes, Chonen, I forgot about him, come, boy, join the dancing!

THE MESSENGER

He's over there.

MAYER

(Looking about, seeing Chonen) He's on the floor, exhausted, asleep.

SENDER

No sleeping tonight, wake him up!

(Mayer tries to wake Chonen, shaking him.)

MAYER

He won't wake up.

(The others gather around Chonen and try to wake him. When they realize what has happened:)

FIRST BATLON

May the Almighty have mercy.

SECOND BATLON

He's dead.

THE MESSENGER

Look at the book in his hand.

THIRD BATLON

From the Kabbalah.

THE MESSENGER

He is destroyed.

Act Two

Three months later. Leah's wedding day. Leah and Fradde in a mikvah. Fradde is holding a sheet while Leah washes herself, preparing for her wedding day.

FRADDE
Now there are three sins for which a woman might die in childbirth, and these are: Not keeping separation when we are bleeding. Not keeping separation for the offering of the first dough. And last, for failing to light the Shabbes candles as a separate blessing. Because in the Talmud it says: "The soul which I have given you is called a candle, and therefore I've given you a commandment concerning candles. If you keep these commandments, well and good—"

LEAH
"—But if not I will take away your soul."

FRADDE
The world is a troubled and mysterious place, don't you think? I think it is a troubled and mysterious place. Well certainly mysterious. And troubled too. I remember a niggun they say was first sung by the wife of the Great Maggid:

(Sings:)

Far away, at one end of the world, the world atop a mountain,
Pouring from a fissure in a stone, a stone, issues a fountain.
At the other ending of the world, the heart of the world is
    found;
The heart adores the fountain, and longs to drink its waters.
If it ever traveled to the spring, the heart of the world would
    die.
The heart must never travel; but watch and long forever.

Forever, never, never to be there!
Never! Never! To breathe your mountain air!
And never drink you in!
Never plunge within!
Ah, thirsty, longing, burning,
The heart forever watching!

Every living thing requires time: in time the spring is living.
Since the spring has no time of its own, its own, the heart is
    giving
To the spring each day a little time, but when the night draws
    nigh,
The spring, afraid of dying, sings to the heart for mercy.
As the heart sings longing in return, another day is made.
Across the world they're calling, with songs of love and mercy.

Oh mercy, mercy, give me one more day!
Minutes, hours, let my waters play!
Oh heart of precious time,
Hear your fountain chime
And grant another morning,
Oh heart forever watching.

As their singing spreads across the world, the world, in threads
    of fire,
Shining threads connecting living hearts, the hearts feel deep
    desire.

Every living creature has a heart, and every heart a thread.
And He of Holy Wisdom draws all the threads together.
From the fiery threads is woven time, and thus new days are
    made;
Unto the heart is given, unto the spring is given.
As the spring pours waters through the days, the heart of the
    world looks on.
And so the world continues, until the world is gone.

The wife of the Great Maggid sang this song the night she conceived Abraham her son, later called Abraham the Angel, because he was so Holy he wasn't a man. When he grew up, Abraham the Angel was too awesome to even look upon, not even his wife could look at him. On their wedding night Abraham the Angel's wife fainted dead away when he came to their bed. But she bore him two sons when she found her courage.

But after that Abraham the Angel lived alone. And so did his wife.

SCENE 2

Three months later, a square in Brinnitz. To the left is the synagogue, its exterior revealing its antiquity in both style and wear. In front of the synagogue, slightly off to one side, is a mound of earth atop which a very old gravestone is inscribed: "HERE LIE THE PURE AND HOLY BRIDE AND BRIDEGROOM, MARTYRED IN THE YEAR 5408 (1648). BLESSED BE THEIR SOULS." To the right is Sender's handsome wooden home, with a gate, a courtyard that stretches around the front and along the side of the house, and a porch. Behind these buildings the alleys and houses, taverns and shops of Brinnitz stretch away to the riverbank. A windmill is visible, as is the brick bathhouse, the poorhouse, and on the other side of the river, dense dark forests.

On a bluff above the river is the Jewish cemetery with many tombstones.

The gates to Sender's house are open. Long tables extend across his courtyard into the town square. At the tables the town's poor population, beggars and cripples, are eating ravenously. Waiters bring heaping platters of food and baskets of bread from Sender's house.

The people of Brinnitz move about the square, the men going in and out of the synagogue with shawls and phylacteries on, the women in and out of Sender's house with food and gifts. Dance music and the sounds of a crowd are heard from the courtyard behind Sender's house.

It's early evening. The Messenger, wearing an elegant long satin frock coat, his hands tucked behind his back in his belt, is examining the grave of the martyred bride and bridegroom, talking to the First and Third Batlonim.

FIRST BEGGAR

A groschen, a kopek, a shekel, a ruble?

SECOND BEGGAR

Give to the poor, you can afford it!

THIRD BEGGAR

It's a special mitzvah, to give money at a wedding.

FOURTH BEGGAR

Make the beggar-angels happy, give me a ruble.

THE MESSENGER

God forbid us we should be talking about graves at a wedding, but it's an unusual thing, isn't it, a grave in the foreyard of a synagogue.

FIRST BATLON

It's from long ago. There were dreadful pogroms here. The cossack chief Chmielnitski, may he burn forever in Hell, even on Shabbes may he burn.

THIRD BATLON

Amen.

THE MESSENGER

"HERE LIE THE PURE AND HOLY BRIDE AND BRIDE-GROOM, MARTYRED IN THE YEAR 5408. BLESSED BE THEIR SOULS."

THIRD BATLON

Well, Amen again.

FIRST BATLON

The cossacks attacked Brinnitz on Easter Sunday, they slaughtered every other person in their path. Hundreds died, including this bride and her bridegroom, just as they were stepping under the chuppah, and the orchestra was playing. After it was over the pair was buried, husband and wife in a single grave, to mingle dust and bones till Moshiach comes, and ever since then the site is holy. Whenever he performs a marriage, our rabbi hears sighs that come from the earth. And people say sometimes a ghostly orchestra is playing. So in Brinnitz we have a custom: after any wedding, the guests dance around the grave, to cheer up the grieving, martyred dead.

THE MESSENGER
I approve of the custom.

(Mayer enters from Sender's yard.)

MAYER
Have you seen such a party as the party he's throwing?

THE MESSENGER
The dead should not be excluded from any celebration.

MAYER
Sholem aleichem! Back in town! More messages to deliver?

THE MESSENGER
I go where they send me.

MAYER
Well you've timed your visit nicely. Here we are having the wedding to end all weddings!

THE MESSENGER
Even in Paradise they're talking about it.

MAYER
(Laughing) Sender thinks he can feed every beggar in Brinnitz! You came by the river road. Did you pass the bridegroom's family on your way?

THE MESSENGER
He'll be here shortly.

MAYER

That's good! They're late!

THE MESSENGER

The bridegroom cometh! He'll be on time.

MAYER

Quick, into the house, have delicious food. Sender, I remember, didn't like you but today, even you will be welcomed! A quarter of a buffle fish and a hunk of roast on every plate, big bowls of carrot soup, and there's cake and honey and real brandy besides. Who knew even Sender had this kind of money?

FIRST BATLON

Sender plays it safe. You have to when you invite the poor to table. Rich guests you know who they are, but a poor guest could be an itinerant tzaddik fond of disguises: the holy ones like to catch the wealthy unawares in the act of being greedy—one of God's thirty-six Just men, one of the lamed vovniks could be in Sender's yard right now!

MAYER

Or even the Prophet Elijah returned could be back there, sitting on a bench, blowing to cool down a spoonful of carrot soup. Didn't Moshiach Himself squat for years outside the gates of Babylon, disguised as a beggar? And He never revealed Himself only because no one thought to ask Him if he was Moshiach, because why would the King of the World sit among lepers, and then He went away, unnoticed and unasked-for, back to Heaven, and look at the trouble we've had ever since. So you have to watch it with the poor.

THE MESSENGER

Not only the poor. All people are entitled to respect, and generosity. We've all had lives before this one, and no one is simply or entirely who he or she appears to be.

A Dybbuk

*(Mayer leads the Messenger and the First and Third Batlonim into
Sender's house, as Leah, wearing her wedding dress, dances on from
the rear courtyard, her partner a poor woman carrying a baby.
Many other poor women, some old, some on crutches, follow closely
behind, clamoring for a turn with the bride.)*

A POOR WOMAN WITH A BABY
I danced with the bride! And so did the baby!

A LAME WOMAN
I danced with her too, she has such cold fingers!

A VERY HOMELY MAN
I hate this custom, why should only the women dance with the
bride, I could make her spin for real, cold fingers or cold feet,
I know ways to make a bride spin!

(Fradde enters onto Sender's porch.)

FRADDE
Leah, stop dancing with the paupers now, darling, they'll make
you dizzy! Gitl! Bessye!

(Gitl and Bessye enter from inside the house.)

FRADDE
Go rescue Leah, she's being danced to death.

A VERY OLD POOR WOMAN
Not yet, not yet, I haven't had my turn.

A POOR WOMAN WITH A BABY
And Yachne so old she's danced with every bride since Eve!

A VERY OLD POOR WOMAN
That's enough, you korva, you pinska, snake-eyes . . .

*(Mayer returns from the house with a chair, and he sits in the
square, mopping his brow.)*

MAYER

(Singing:)

Rich papa Sender, avoiding a sin,
Asks beggars and bridegrooms and messengers in!
With rubles and groschen and kopeks in store
For every poor soul who can squeeze through his door!

Sender's got money, a crown for his head,
Rents homes to the living and graves to the dead,
Sells vodka to cossacks, lends gold to the czar,
Knows just who his friends and his enemies are:
His friends are his debtors, all shabby and slim,
And his enemies: those who lend money to him!

THE POOR

(Joining Mayer, singing:)

Zlotys turn rubles when they cross his palms
And the angels in paradise offer him psalms—
Collateral payment when begging for loans.
And even Ha-Shem, on His seven gold thrones,
It's whispered is now one of Reb Sender's debtors;
Ha-Shem has been forced to pawn several letters:
Bet, gimel, dalet, chey, yud and tet!
If the Holy One borrows, who isn't in debt?
We all are, and someday Reb Sender will own
All Brinnitz, the earth, and the Almighty's Throne!

MAYER

Rich papa Sender, obeying the Law
Pries open his purse dropping coins from his craw,
Which leaves his craw free so he's able to pray
For blessings for Leah on her Wedding Day!

*(There is a mad dash and much commotion, all the poor fighting
their way into Sender's house. Only Gitl, Bessye, Leah, Fradde and
the Very Old Poor Woman are left outside. The Very Old Poor
Woman grabs Leah and begins to dance with her.)*

A VERY OLD POOR WOMAN

I need no food or money now, I'm too old to eat or buy things,
only dancing's what I want now, dancing like I used to do, wild
wedding dancing 'round the square and 'round the square, till
the houses spin and the shops spin and the carts and the horses
and the goats spin up and the synagogue whirls like a top and
all of Brinnitz lifts, up, up, into the woozy yellow sky, and the
river's in the air and the cobblestones float like clouds, and I
am as young as you are Leah, and you're even older than me!

*(Gitl intervenes, stopping the dancing pair. Gitl pries the old woman
away.)*

A VERY OLD POOR WOMAN

No! More, please! More please! Not yet, don't take me yet!

(Bessye supports Leah as Gitl leads the old woman away.)

FRADDE

Leah, you're bone-white and worn out, come sit on the porch.

LEAH

I'm fine, I'm fine.

BESSYE

They've dirtied your gown! It's spoiled!

GITL

Let's get rags and wipe it clean before . . .

LEAH

(In a faraway voice) Don't leave me alone, if you leave a bride
alone unmarried, the envious ones on the Other Side . . . *(She
laughs)*

FRADDE

Leah, are you out of your mind, darling, don't talk about evil
things on your wedding day! Spit!

(Fradde, Bessye and Gitl spit.)

FRADDE

Twice more!

(Fradde, Bessye and Gitl spit twice more.)

LEAH

My mouth's gone dry, they danced the spit out of me, their need was so overwhelming everything flowed out of me, warmth and wetness, I dried, I felt airborne like an old tamarind husk on the wind . . .

FRADDE

Leah, darling . . .

LEAH

The souls of the Other Side are everywhere, Fradde, and your spitting doesn't worry them, because they aren't evil, only dead, cut down while still young, and there are so many of them, so many everywhere, bodies buried everywhere, souls of the dead in the air . . .

FRADDE

Souls of the righteous rest in the bright lights of Paradise, Leahlah, they're up on high, not here in Brinnitz, which is only for the living, and those who don't belong.

(Fradde spits.
The Messenger enters and stands unobtrusively apart.)

FRADDE

Now come inside, rest yourself, eat something warm . . .

LEAH

What about the ones who have been cheated of long lives, what about the ones who die too soon? What becomes of everything they were supposed to do, the tears unshed, the happy days never spent in happiness? The children they never had together, all of that, does all that unspent life have no place to go? Once upon a time there was a boy with a great mind and a soul as tall as the towers of Jerusalem, oh he was beautiful and he would have been beautiful for ninety years more, but he died while he was still a boy, in an instant he was dead. They put him in the ground, in earth that wasn't ready to receive him, with prayers on his lips he never had time to pray, and words for people he didn't have the breath to speak. Fradde, blow a candle out and if it's still tall and straight you simply light it again, you don't throw it out; if a life is extinguished before its vessel has grown frail and broken, it can't be forever, its flame can be rekindled.

FRADDE
Leah, my only darling, it's your wedding day and you shouldn't be thinking about anyone but the bridegroom, and nothing unhappy, and God forbid nothing unholy, for only Alvinu Malchenu knows why anything is.

LEAH
My mother died young. She didn't even have time to know why she was put here on earth, and then she was taken. Fradde, I want to go to the cemetery now and invite mother to come to my wedding, to wait with my father by the chuppah and lead the marital procession, and then dance with me like we did when I was very small. I've seen her, Fradde, on the Holy Days, on the Festivals, at Pesach she watches us from the cold without, hoping to be asked in . . . The dead will talk to you if you permit them; this martyred couple, the holy bride and bridegroom, they visit me night after night, and they were young and terribly beautiful and each was bursting with joy when they stepped under the canopy, and the music was so joyful it hid the clatter of horses' hooves, and the scent from the baking ovens was so sweet it masked the devil's stench, and the first stroke of the axe scattered his teeth across the square, and the horses' hooves tore through her dress as she ran, and they seized her veil with their hands and . . .

GITL

Leah, stop! It's horrible!

FRADDE

Leah, come in and lie down till your bridegroom arrives—
where do you suppose he could . . .

LEAH

Holy bride and bridegroom! I invite you to my wedding! Come
stand with me under the canopy, stand close so I can feel you
near me . . .

*(There is a sudden blast of wedding music from a klezmer orches-
tra. All four women scream, and Leah nearly faints.)*

GITL

It's alright, it's alright, it's the bridegroom finally arrived! Leah,
we'll go see what he's like.

FRADDE

You're supposed to tell her only one thing: black hair or blond!

BESSYE

Is it alright, Leah?

(Leah nods yes.)

GITL

Come on!

(Gitl and Bessye run off. The Messenger approaches Leah.)

THE MESSENGER

Bride.

LEAH

What . . . ? *(Leah stares at him)* What do you want?

THE MESSENGER

Let me tell you something; I speak with a certain authority. The souls of the dead are everywhere, as you say, but souls always seek bodies, because only through the flesh can a soul purify itself. Some souls must pass through a number of bodies before they are cleansed.

Sinful souls, bride, enter the bodies of beasts of the ground, birds of the air, even plants, and there, unable to achieve holiness, they await a tzaddik, who sees their plight, and sets them free. Some souls enter the bodies of infants, and by doing good in their new lives they ascend.

LEAH

I understand.

THE MESSENGER

And then there are souls, troubled and dark, without a home or resting place, and these attempt to enter the body of another person, and even these are trying to ascend.

(Sender calls from inside his house.)

SENDER

Leah, come, the bridegroom's finally arrived!

THE MESSENGER

And such a soul is called a dybbuk.

(The Messenger vanishes. Leah doesn't move. Sender enters.)

SENDER

Leah!

FRADDE

She's catching her breath, she danced with the poor and they wore her out, let her rest her nerves, she's nervous.

SENDER

It's a mitzvah to dance with the poor and to feed them. *(He looks at the sky)* The sky's already dark, we have to start soon.

FRADDE

She hasn't gone to the graveyard yet.

(Sender goes to Leah.)

SENDER

Go to your mother, my darling daughter, we'll wait, tell her Sender is waiting for her, to hold her hand at her daughter's wedding. Let her see the fine Jewish woman I raised up in you, and bid her to come meet your husband, who is a student, and respectful, and from a very good family with marvelous connections.

(Sender wipes his tears away, kisses Leah and returns to the house.)

LEAH

There's someone else in the graveyard Fradde, and I want to invite him too.

FRADDE

You ask only Mother and your grandpa and your aunt Mirele may they shine in Paradise. The dead are lonely and if you start asking other than family, the ones who don't get asked get jealous and angry.

LEAH

Just one other.

FRADDE

Really Leah I'm scared to do that. You know the talk, they say he died in uncleanliness, in horrible sin, his grave isn't even marked. Nobody knows where it is.

LEAH

I know where he's buried. He's told me where.

FRADDE

God protect us.

LEAH

He asked that I invite him tonight.

(Gitl and Bessye enter.)

BESSYE

He's here!

GITL

I saw him!

BESSYE

Blond hair!

GITL

No, jet black!

BESSYE

Blond!

GITL

Let's go look again.

(They exit.
Leah starts to leave in the opposite direction.)

FRADDE

Leah, wait for Fradde, next you'll be wanting to go there alone, such a strange girl . . .

(They exit. The stage is momentarily empty, and gloomy.
Music, and then Nachman, father of the bridegroom; Rabbi

Mendl, the bridegroom's teacher; and Menashe, the bridegroom,
tiny, pigeon-chested, pop-eyes like a newt's. The bridegroom's fam-
ily—his mother, aunts, uncles and cousins follow after. Sender
comes out of the house to greet them.)

SENDER

Sholem aleichem Reb Nachman and family! Welcome,
Menashe, Rabbi Mendl, Mrs. Nachman, everyone welcome!

(Kisses and handshakes all around.)

SENDER

Reb Nachman my friend you're terribly late! We worried.

NACHMAN

You wouldn't believe this trip! We were on the river road but
it seems to have doubled in length and forked many times since
I was last on it, which was only last month. And the roadbed
has fallen into disrepair, at one point it just vanishes into a great
marsh that wasn't there before, we were almost stuck for the
night. My wife says that demons, God should protect us, were
trying to keep us out of Brinnitz.

MRS. NACHMAN

Demons! Pooh pooh pooh!

NACHMAN

But I have a seasoned and determined team of mules, mules
with fire in their nostrils and with demon-defying spirits.

SENDER

Perhaps you need to rest a bit, before . . .

MRS. NACHMAN

Oh no, there's too much to tie up, the dowry contract, the dis-
tribution of gifts, the rabbi's fees, the cantor and the beadle
and the orchestra. The fathers must talk!

A Dybbuk

(The two fathers walk up and down the square, transacting.)

RABBI MENDL

(To Menashe) Menashe, remember, during the meal you're to sit quietly at the table, don't fidget, don't squirm, eat the food, don't leave and wander off, or I'll kill you. And keep your eyes down, you're supposed to, don't bug about the room the way you do. As soon as they've cleared the dishes the shammes gets up and says: "The bridegroom will commence his Talmudic exegesis," and you are to recite the whole story letter-perfect . . .

MENASHE

"Holy Rabbi Meir had a wise wife named Beruria, and she had a light-headed sister who . . ."

RABBI MENDL

Yes, exactly, not now, after they take the plates away, stand on your chair, sing out in a manly voice, the louder the better, and remember, letter-perfect, or I'll kill you. Don't be frightened. MENASHE! You hear me?!?

MENASHE

Rabbi. I *am* frightened.

RABBI MENDL

Of what? You know everything, I taught you, did you forget your Talmudic exegesis?

MENASHE

I remember, but . . .

RABBI MENDL

But what?

MENASHE

The journey here was so scary. And everyone's *staring* at me like I'm a gypsy's monkey. I hate the eyes of strange people, I hate being stared at.

RABBI MENDL

That's your Aunt Rochele's evil eye at work, but I gave you an amulet . . .

MENASHE

And mostly Rebbe I am afraid of her! That girl! I've had dreams, she's terrifying, I shouldn't have come here, I want to hide in a burrow in the ground, Rebbe, I . . . *(He sees the grave of the Holy Couple) Rebbe! It's a grave!* What sort of people put a grave in their town square? I don't want to be married Rebbe, when we thank God in the morning he didn't make us women, no one's more grateful than I am, Rebbe, I don't want to get married, I'm ugly, she has terrible burning eyes, I don't . . .

RABBI MENDL

Menashe! You're to stop this immediately! Or you'll forget your speech and you'll make me look stupid! Come, let's rehearse.

(A Tall Pale Woman, A Very Old Poor Woman, A Poor Woman with a Baby, A Very Homely Man and the other poor people enter from Sender's feast. They've eaten, and they're melancholy. As they cross the square heading back to their homes and the poorhouse:)

A TALL PALE WOMAN

The instant you finish eating, all that lies ahead of you is days of not enough to eat.

A POOR WOMAN WITH A BABY

It was a decent meal, though they made such a fuss you'd think we were each getting a whole calf.

A VERY OLD POOR WOMAN

To me it's no matter. I only eat now to make of myself a bigger meal for the worms . . .

A VERY HOMELY MAN

The bride disappeared. And did you notice they'd cut each roll in half?

A Dybbuk

A POOR WOMAN WITH A BABY
He's the richest Chasid in the district, and he couldn't manage a whole roll for each guest. The rich guests got rolls.

A VERY HOMELY MAN
The rich guests got geese, and lamb, and clear broth.

A VERY OLD POOR WOMAN
I had a nice fast dance with the bride. A strange girl. Sitting next to me at the table was the Prophet Elijah. Dressed for the poorhouse. He ate and left. I'll be dead soon. God willing.

(It has gotten very dark. The lights in the shops and taverns and houses are going out. In the synagogue, as the poor cross the square, someone is lighting many candles, and many candles are lit in Sender's home. Sender, Gitl and Bessye come out on Sender's porch, looking anxiously into the gathering dark.)

SENDER
Where on earth is my daughter? What could be keeping her, what could she be thinking? And Fradde, a responsible woman! How can a visit to a graveyard take so long? They should be back, God forbid anything's happened.

BESSYE
There they are!

GITL
Let's go meet them!

(Fradde enters the square, and behind her, Leah.)

SENDER
Well *finally!*

FRADDE
Oh Sender, forgive me, we're so terribly sorry, I'll never listen to your daughter again!

SENDER

What happened to you?

(Women come out of Sender's house, including Mrs. Nachman.)

MRS. NACHMAN

The bride must come in now, she has to bless the Shabbes candles.

(The women and Leah go inside. Fradde talks to Bessye and Gitl.)

FRADDE

She fainted. Look! I'm still shaking from the fright, I tried to wake her, I thought she'd died.

BESSYE

She's fasting, she fasts all the time now, she's weak and she faints a lot.

FRADDE

She shouldn't fast except on her wedding day! It's like she's disappearing more and more, she's not sitting shiva, she's a bride.

GITL

Did she faint at her mother's grave?

FRADDE

No, it was another grave, unmarked, and don't ask me what happened, don't ask me what happened, don't ask me what happened, it's best not to know.

(Leah is brought from the house by the women. She's seated on a decorated chair. The klezmer orchestra strikes up wedding music. Menashe, Rabbi Mendl and Nachman enter from across the square, followed by the bridegroom's party. Menashe carries a bridal veil in his hands. He goes to Leah and places the veil atop her head, and brings it down over her face. The Messenger comes out of the synagogue.)

A Dybbuk

Leah stands, tears off the bridal veil and throws it aside, pushes Menashe away, and screams:)

LEAH

You are not my bridegroom!

(Everyone is horrified. Sender, Fradde and Leah's friends rush to Leah. Sender grabs Leah.)

SENDER

Leah! My love! What's wrong?

(Leah tears free and runs to the grave of the Holy Couple. She throws herself on the grave, clawing at the earth.)

LEAH

Save me, Holy Bride and Groom!

(The others run to Leah and lift her up. She becomes wild-eyed and pulls away from them, and then screams in a strange, male voice:)

LEAH

AAAAAAAHHHHHHH! AAAAAAHHHHHHH! YOU BURIED ME! BUT NOW I'VE COME BACK TO MY BELOVED, AND I'LL NEVER LEAVE HER AGAIN!

(Sender goes to his daughter. She roars in his face:)

LEAH

MURDERER!

NACHMAN

She's gone mad!

THE MESSENGER

A dybbuk has entered the body of the bride.

Act Three

SCENE 1

Miropol; two days later. A train station near the Jewish Ghetto.
People are disembarking from a train, only just arrived. Among
them, the Messenger.

FIRST PASSENGER
It's a miracle! Two days from Krakow to Tarnopol to Miropol!
Home! In Two days! Used to take a week.

SECOND PASSENGER
And an even greater miracle! They let Jews ride the thing!

THIRD PASSENGER
I find the insistent tempo of the wheels and pistons, the humming of the rails, the sway of the cabin and the hiss of the steam extraordinarily conducive to contemplation, and to prayer. I prayed all the way from Cheroszchev.

FIRST PASSENGER
From such an invention, only good can ever come.

THE MESSENGER
Blessed be He from whom all inventions come.

SECOND PASSENGER

So how goes it with a Jew?

THE MESSENGER

So how should it go?

SECOND PASSENGER

So what brings you to Miropol? You're not a Chasid.

THE MESSENGER

Just a messenger. At the house of your Rabbi Azriel . . .

THIRD PASSENGER

Of Blessed Name.

FIRST PASSENGER

A righteous man, a tzaddik.

THE MESSENGER

. . . a girl has been brought, possessed by a dybbuk.

THIRD PASSENGER

Sssshhhhhhh!

SECOND PASSENGER

Oh, preposterous!

THIRD PASSENGER

Don't speak of such things in public! They won't let us ride the train if they hear us talking about . . .

SECOND PASSENGER

And you believe that stuff? A dybbuk? And to see that, you came all the way from . . . let me guess. Minsk.

THE MESSENGER

Much farther than Minsk.

SECOND PASSENGER

Farther than Minsk! You've wasted your time and your money.
God save the credulous. A dybbuk! He rode the train to see
the dybbuk!

FIRST PASSENGER

Ever been to Moscow?

THE MESSENGER

(Shaking his head) Not on my route.

FIRST PASSENGER

In Moscow now they have electric lighting! And fantastically
long wires, threads of fire, just like in the legends, radiant
threads stretching from Moscow to St. Petersburg! Along
which words fly, faster than the angels fly, over the earth, words
of electric fire, like chittering crickets, can you imagine.

THIRD PASSENGER

When Moshiach comes He will arrive by train, with a first-class
ticket.

FIRST PASSENGER

And light in the evening, electrical light.

SECOND PASSENGER

Soon we won't need candles anymore. In a world without candles, there will be no more dybbuks. There will be fewer hys-
terical women. With dybbuks, it's always women, have you
noticed?

THE MESSENGER

If you say so. It is hard for me to believe such things are possible. But I have never been to Moscow. Which way to Rabbi
Azriel's house?

THIRD PASSENGER

Go first to the ghetto. You can find it by the smell. Anyone
there will direct you.

SECOND PASSENGER

I hate the smell of candle smoke. Give me electric light. In a
world of electric light, even Jews can ride the trains.

SCENE 2

A large room in Rabbi Azriel's house. On the right is a door lead-ing to other rooms. Near the door is a small Holy Ark and a read-ing stand. On the rear wall, the front door of the house is flanked by benches and windows. To the left is a broad table. At the head of the table is an armchair. Near the Ark are a small table, a sofa and reading chairs.

Rabbi Azriel of Miropol sits in the armchair, facing the outside door. Michl, the gabbe (manager), stands at the table behind the armchair. At a table nearby sits a young man, the Scribe of Rabbi Azriel, who records the proceeding of the court in a book. Sender and Fradde stand inside near the door. Leah stands at the thresh-old, refusing to enter the room.

It's Saturday night, shortly after the maariv (evening prayers)

SENDER

Leah, have pity on your miserable father, don't shame him before the rabbi.

FRADDE

Please Leah, obey your father, come into the room.

LEAH

I want to but I can't.

RABBI AZRIEL

Leah! I order you to enter!

(Leah enters and goes to the Rabbi's table.)

RABBI AZRIEL

Sit down.

(Leah sits, but almost immediately jumps up again and shouts in the male voice:)

LEAH

Leave me in peace! I don't want to be here!

(Leah tries to run to the front door, but Sender and Fradde grab her.)

RABBI AZRIEL

Dybbuk, I command you: Tell me who you are.

THE DYBBUK

Rabbi of Miropol! You know all too well who I am! The others don't need my name.

RABBI AZRIEL

I ask not for your name, Dybbuk: Who are you?

(Little pause.)

THE DYBBUK

A wanderer. Who once sought a new road.

RABBI AZRIEL

There's only one road and that is righteousness.

THE DYBBUK

Too narrow! It would not take me where I belonged. There are other roads, for larger souls than yours.

RABBI AZRIEL

And you roamed those roads. With your large soul. And couldn't find your way home again. But you know the Torah: the dead may not dwell among the living.

THE DYBBUK

I never died!

RABBI AZRIEL

You have, and you must leave the body of this girl.

THE DYBBUK

I am her bridegroom; God ordained this; we are meant to be.

RABBI AZRIEL

Listen to me, wanderer: you have died, and only after the Holy Shofar is sounded on the great and terrible day of Judgment, of Wrath and Awe, only then may you return to the daylight world. Now leave her body: you blight a living branch of the eternal tree of the people Israel.

THE DYBBUK

Rabbi of Miropol! I've heard the stories about your strength! Command the angels to circle overhead, but you cannot shackle me! I've no place else to go, every ascent is barred, every doorway bolted against me! I can only fall from here into the hands of waiting demons. I cannot leave!

(Leah kneels before the Rabbi.)

THE DYBBUK

There is heaven and there is earth and there are uncountable worlds throughout the universe but nowhere, anywhere is there a resting place for me. I've found shelter, here, and you want to drive me out into the night. Have mercy, have pity on me, don't banish me.

RABBI AZRIEL

Homeless one, I do pity you, your suffering shreds my heart, and if I can I will rescue you, from the demons and from the Devil himself. But you must leave the body of the girl.

THE DYBBUK

I WILL NEVER LEAVE!

RABBI AZRIEL

Go, Michl, send to the synagogue, ask Rabbi Shimshin to come to me. Find a quorum of men and bring them here.

(Michl exits.)

RABBI AZRIEL

Dybbuk! Soul of a man who has left this world! I, Azriel, son of my righteous mother Hadas, order you to leave the body of the girl Leah, daughter of Channa, and I order you to harm no living creature as you depart! If you comply, I will protect you from the Sitra-Achra—my power can accomplish that. Refuse me, and I will blast you with curses and the awful power of God, I will with my outstretched arm hurl anathema at you and leave you to your unimaginable fate alone on the Other Side.

THE DYBBUK

(Screaming) Nothing can expel me! No power rescue me! No heaven is worth more to me than here where I am! No hell half as terrible as leaving her!

SENDER

(With supplicant arms) Rabbi, tzaddik, my daughter, help me, save her, she's my only child!

RABBI AZRIEL

What is this, Sender? How did this come to pass?

SENDER

Two days ago, just as the bridegroom placed the veil on her head, she . . .

RABBI AZRIEL

That's not the question and you know it. Through what flaw did the Evil One gain entrance?

SENDER

Rabbi, I swear my Leah is a pure and decent Jewish girl, she . . .

Act Three

RABBI AZRIEL

The Lord visits his wrath across generations.

(Sender looks at the Scribe, who is busy writing.)

SENDER

Rabbi, must this boy write down everything we say?

RABBI AZRIEL

He must! Yes, absolutely, we record the nocturnal doings of God the same as the miracles and blessings He bestows; the tales of the dybbukim are as important as the legends of the tzaddikim, and as instructive. It may be that your daughter suffers this evil impregnation simply so that we may turn her sufferings into a text—for others to study in the ages to come. Or it may be that she suffers for some other reason. Children sometimes bear the punishment for their parents' wickedness.

SENDER

Don't you think I haven't asked myself a dozen times every minute: What have I done to God that suddenly He should hate me so ferociously He would smite my only joy with . . .

RABBI AZRIEL

Have you asked the dybbuk?

SENDER

You can't ask him anything, he only rages and snarls.

THE DYBBUK

MURDERER!

SENDER

You see?

THE DYBBUK

EVIL ANCIENT MURDERER! WHAT I'M SUFFERING MAY YOU ENDURE A THOUSANDFOLD! MAY YOU

NEVER FIND REST! MAY YOUR MONEY POISON
YOUR BLOOD!

SENDER

I recognize his voice, it belonged to a yeshiva student who
studied in Brinnitz, he perished in shul a few months ago.
He'd profaned, he was studying forbidden things, his soul had
grown rusted and corroded, deformed.

RABBI AZRIEL

How is it you know so intimately the state of his soul?

SENDER

Right before he died, Rabbi, he told a fellow student that sin
came from God, God help us, that we weakened ourselves
fighting the devil. He was an alchemist, he read the Zohar, the
Book of Raziel which Adam mislaid, he would chew and swal-
low scraps of paper inscribed with spells, he made a strange
powder by crushing pearls and he recited the seven colors of
gold, he told his friend he was making gold coins for some
wicked old miser.

RABBI AZRIEL

You knew this student well, Sender?

SENDER

No, he was occasionally a guest at my table for Shabbes, I've
always had students at my table.

RABBI AZRIEL

Think Sender, till your brains ache, did you insult this boy? Did
he have bad table manners, did you mock him? Refuse him
food when he was hungry?

SENDER

Never.

RABBI AZRIEL

Have you injured anyone in his family?

SENDER

I don't even know his family name, Rabbi, I never spoke to the boy, I can't remember, please help me, I'm not perfect but I'm a decent man, I . . .

RABBI AZRIEL

They tell me you don't read so much anymore, Sender; your eyes are faded from adding sums and keeping accounts.

(Michl enters with the quorum of men.)

THE DYBBUK

I WILL NOT LEAVE!

RABBI AZRIEL

(To the men of the quorum) Holy minyan. In your names and in your powers, do you invest me with the authority to expel from the body of this Jewish girl a spirit who refuses to leave her of its own free will?

THE MINYAN

(Unison) In our names and in our powers we invest you, Rabbi Azriel, with the authority to expel from the body of this Jewish girl a spirit who refuses to leave her of its own free will.

(The Rabbi stands.)

RABBI AZRIEL

In the name of Almighty God, I beseech you, one last time, leave the body of this girl. If you refuse me I will excommunicate you and bind your soul over to the angels of destruction.

(A terrifying pause.)

THE DYBBUK

In the name of God Almighty, I am with my intended now, and I will never leave her.

RABBI AZRIEL

Michl. Bring a white robe for every person in the room, seven rams' horns and seven black candles.

(Michl goes into the inner room.)

LEAH

(As if waking, in her own voice) Fradde! What are they doing to him? What are they going to do to me?

FRADDE

Hush, child, the rabbi only wishes you well.

SENDER

Rabbi Azriel is among the holiest of men, Leah, he . . .

LEAH

Fradde, please, tell him . . . I want to leave here . . . Don't tell him anything. Tell him to leave me alone.

FRADDE

Sleep, my poor child, close your eyes. The rabbi's very wise and only good can come from him.

LEAH

Hold me, Fradde . . .

FRADDE

I *can't*, my only love. You terrify me . . .

(Michl returns, carrying the rams' horns and the candles. Behind him, the Messenger carries the white robes. Behind them is Rabbi Shimshin.)

RABBI SHIMSHIN

A good week, blessed Rebbe.

RABBI AZRIEL

(Standing) And a good year, Rabbi. Michl has told you . . . ?

RABBI SHIMSHIN

He has.

RABBI AZRIEL

The spirit refuses to abdicate, there's no choice but to drive him out this girl, violently. Before I proceed, you, as Chief Rabbi of Miropol, must give your consent, and the mitzvah of sparing her young life will shine in your crown in heaven.

RABBI SHIMSHIN

Rabbi, I am your disciple in all things, but excommunication is a terrible fate for a Jewish soul, and Rabbi . . . When Michl told me what had befallen Sender's daughter I was only very frightened, not surprised, because in this past week I have had three dreams which clearly pertain to this case.

RABBI AZRIEL

If we are to perform this ceremony, Rabbi Shimshin, it must be done before midnight as you know, and . . . There is a danger here. The child is dying. The dybbuk is drawing away her life.

RABBI SHIMSHIN

I cannot consent to an exorcism until we speak.

(Little pause.)

RABBI AZRIEL

(To Michl) Rabbi Shimshin and I will confer.
(Turning to the minyan) Pray to the Blessed Name for mercy, or wisdom, or protection; do not touch the girl or let her touch you.

(Azriel takes Shimshin aside. They confer in whispers. The minyan begins its prayers, everyone shukkeling. The First Chasid stops and says:)

FIRST CHASID

I can't pray. I am afraid.

SECOND CHASID

Pray anyway. If you pray, the Holy One, Blessed be He, may preserve you from Evil; if Evil overtakes you, it's better that it overtake you while you're praying.

THIRD CHASID

So said my rabbi while they were burning our village. Every murdered man was found wearing his tefilin and talis. We buried them that way, in a big hasty pit. And then we fled into the forests. It was night, I was a child, I remember owls screeching.

FIRST CHASID

The darkness and misery of the world is incomprehensible to me. I cannot pray.

THIRD CHASID

The world is in its last age. If Moshiach doesn't come soon there'll be no Jews left to welcome Him.

(Azriel and Shimshin cease their conference.)

RABBI AZRIEL

Take the girl to a room.

FRADDE

Rabbi, I am terribly afraid, she's cold, and hardly breathing, and she won't open her eyes.

RABBI AZRIEL

The room is cold, the world is cold, its variety is deceptive, there's not so much to see. Heaven preserve her.

(Fradde leads Leah out, accompanied by Michl.)

SENDER

Where's she going? Rabbi, why aren't you . . .

RABBI AZRIEL

(To the minyan) Everyone, retire to my study. Pray. This house must vibrate to the sound of praying. I will call you in an hour.

(The minyan leaves. Rabbi Shimshin notices the Scribe, who is writing everything down.)

RABBI SHIMSHIN

If these proceedings are being recorded, the scribe should wear an amulet or a tefilin on his arm as he writes. In Baghdad only recently the scribes who made the records of the dybbuk infestation that was the false messiah, Sabbathai Zvi . . .

(Everyone except Azriel spits.)

RABBI SHIMSHIN

The scribes themselves became possessed by the false messiah, merely by writing the letters of his name.

RABBI AZRIEL

Almighty God, assist me, I'm your servant, don't hinder me, strengthen me. I will proceed towards that which I know to be Just. Illumine this night. Do not leave me in such blindness. Sender?

SENDER

Yes, Rebbe?

RABBI AZRIEL

Have you remembered anything, Sender, about this dead boy, anything that might help save your daughter?

SENDER

Rebbe, I can't think clearly, I . . .

RABBI AZRIEL

Sender surely you remember a young Chasid from Brinnitz who twenty years ago studied here with you? Nissin ben Rivka was his name.

(Little pause.)

SENDER

Nissin died, Rebbe.

RABBI SHIMSHIN

That is true.

RABBI AZRIEL

I remember him, Sender. You were the closest of friends.

SENDER

Nissin moved far away, Rebbe, we lost touch, and I heard he died young.

RABBI SHIMSHIN

For three nights Nissin has appeared to me in my dreams.

SENDER

He's dead.

RABBI SHIMSHIN

Nissin ben Rivka has appeared imploring me to bring Sender of Brinnitz before a Rabbinical Court. Nissin said Sender had spilled Nissin's blood.

SENDER

Lies! I've taken nothing of his! He has no claim on anything that's mine!

RABBI SHIMSHIN

The dead boy who has become a dybbuk is Nissin's son.

(Pause.)

SENDER

(Broken, to Azriel) Rebbe, advise me, tell me what I should do.

RABBI AZRIEL

We will summon the righteous dead man Nissin ben Rivka to present his charges before our court. It's his right as a Jew. You'll hear the charges brought before the court, what else Sender. You have no right to refuse. Sender?

SENDER

I obey.

RABBI AZRIEL

You summoned the bridegroom and his family, Sender?

SENDER

Rebbe, I think the bridegroom's family is having second thoughts about being my in-laws. I think they will refuse to come.

RABBI AZRIEL

I ORDER THEM TO BE HERE, I COMMAND IT! *(Roaring at Sender!)* HAAAAAAA! The bridegroom must be here!

(The Messenger enters.)

THE MESSENGER

The bridegroom will arrive in time.

(Rabbi Azriel looks at the Messenger.)

RABBI AZRIEL

There's a stranger in our midst.

SENDER

He's a messenger, Rebbe, he . . . *(To the Messenger)* You were there, that night, when . . .

RABBI AZRIEL

Has he delivered his message, Sender?

SENDER

I . . . I don't know, Rabbi, I . . . Should I ask him to leave, Rabbi?

RABBI AZRIEL

God forbid! Welcome the outsider, offer him a chair.

SENDER

No, Rebbe, this man is strange, I think he . . .

RABBI AZRIEL

Sender . . . Can a few short years really have changed a man so much?
(To the Messenger, gesturing to Sender) You see how frail we are?
(To Sender) You don't welcome the stranger, you remember nothing, you question nothing, you're joyless . . .

SENDER

Joyless? My daughter is destroyed, everything I worked for is destroyed, of course I'm joyless! From what conceivable cause in the world might joy come to . . .

RABBI AZRIEL

Sender! Who made the World?

SENDER

What? Rabbi, please, I don't know what you're asking, I'm . . . miserable, Rebbe, don't ask me difficult questions.

RABBI AZRIEL

Who made the world is a difficult question?

(Little pause.)

SENDER

Please, Rebbe. I am a heartbroken man.

RABBI AZRIEL

Ssssshhh. Sender. I gave you a task. Now go and do what I say.

(Sender exits. Rabbi Azriel turns to the Messenger. They stare at one another; the Messenger smiles. The Rabbi asks him:)

RABBI AZRIEL

So who made the World?

THE MESSENGER

God made the World.

RABBI AZRIEL

The world is Holy because it is from God.

THE MESSENGER

The world is Holy because it is from God.

RABBI AZRIEL

So simple. So wonderful. And yet . . . *(Indicating the direction in which Sender has exited)* You see . . . ? Not so simple. Which is the Holiest of lands?

THE MESSENGER

The Holy Land.

RABBI AZRIEL

The Holiest City?

THE MESSENGER

Jerusalem.

RABBI AZRIEL

The Temple in Jerusalem was the Holiest place, and the Holiest room was?

THE MESSENGER

The Holy of Holies.

RABBI AZRIEL
There are seventy nations, and which is Holiest?

THE MESSENGER
The people Israel.
Of the twelve tribes of Israel the Holiest is Levi,
Of the Levites the Holiest are the priests,
And the Holiest of these is the High Priest of Israel.

RABBI AZRIEL
Three hundred and fifty-four are the days of the year, and
which is Holiest?

THE MESSENGER
Yom Kippur.

RABBI AZRIEL
And which is the Holiest Yom Kippur?

THE MESSENGER
When Yom Kippur falls on Shabbes.

RABBI AZRIEL
Seventy languages are spoken on earth and the Holiest is
Hebrew. That Hebrew is Holiest which is found . . . ?

THE MESSENGER
In the Torah.

RABBI AZRIEL
In the Torah which is the Holiest text?

THE SCRIBE
The Ten Commandments.

RABBI AZRIEL
And which is the Holiest word therein?

THE MESSENGER

(Softly) The Holiest word is the Shem ha-Mfoyrosh.

RABBI AZRIEL

God's own unutterable name.

(Little pause.)

And this is what everyone knows: at one instant all these con-join—on Yom Kippur on Shabbes the High Priest entered the Holy of Holies and pronounced the Shem ha-Mfoyrosh, the Tetragrammaton: Yud, Hey, Vov, Hey. At that moment of complete and absolute holiness, had a single thought of sin, God forbid, a machshovve zorre, entered the mind of the High Priest, the world would have died. Wheresoever a man raises his eyes to heaven, that is the Holy of Holies. Every person created by God, b'tsalmoy uchd'musoy, in His image, is High Priest. Every day of our lives is The Day of Atonement, every day is the Holy Shabbes day, every word spoken without malice is the Shem ha-Vawyaw, the name of God. Therefore, as everyone knows, every sin committed or imagined, every injustice destroys the world. Every word, every thought, every instant of every day. It all comes to rest . . .

(The Messenger lightly touches the nape of the Rabbi's neck.)

RABBI AZRIEL

Yes, there. When a soul falls, when it stumbles under the weight, from the lips of every angel, the Matriarchs and Patriarchs, every tzaddik, from every Holy Ark in every Temple, even from the Almighty Himself, dark lamentations issue forth, drowning the world in woe.

It's a great burden, don't you think? For the joyless and the frail.

THE MESSENGER

The soul is drawn to the Divine Fire like a baby to its mother's breast, but even as it reaches the highest spheres, the Evil One may emerge and, God help his children, the soul will plummet, and of course if it has soared high it will have that much farther to fall.

RABBI AZRIEL
God made the World.

THE MESSENGER
The World is Holy, because it is from God.

THE SCRIBE
I beg your pardon, Rebbe, but last night I had bad dreams, and tonight after Shabbes prayers I found that somehow all my pens were ruined overnight, and now, when I try to write down what you say, the paper won't take the ink.

RABBI AZRIEL
(To the Scribe) Later, perhaps, we'll interpret your dreams and buy new pens and paper. It's all been written before, everything we do and say, it's all in some scroll, some codex, some tractate or holy book—Jews have merely tumbled from the pages of books, what we speak and think has all been written by the Hand of God. From whence comes our joy.

(Offstage, the sonorous sound of a large number of men praying together. Amidst the prayers, a terrible wailing sound, equally balanced between grief and rage. A cantor is heard, keening a prayer.)

RABBI AZRIEL
Suddenly I am enormously weary.

RABBI SHIMSHIN
The task of summoning a dead man to Rabbinical Court is very difficult, and very dangerous, and only someone as mighty in his faith as you are could attempt it, Holy Azriel.

RABBI AZRIEL
(To the Scribe) Write the Sh'ma and the blessings, over and

over, till we return, and do not look up from the Book. If a strange thought enters you as you labor, do not dismiss it but write it down. Begin with the bad dream you had last night. And then write Chelmo tovo chozze.

THE SCRIBE

Chelmo tovo chozze.

RABBI SHIMSHIN

Chelmo tovo chazeyso. We have dreamt good dreams.

(As the Scribe writes and mutters the prayers:)

RABBI AZRIEL

I am very weary, and I'm very weak, and older than my days, I have been Rebbe for more than forty years and there are many days when the Almighty hides from me, and I pray to a void, to a fear. I want to seek after my elusive God in silence and contemplation, but there are always petitioners at my door, even on the bad days when I am abandoned and empty. Many generations have passed since the Temple fell, and I am as many miles from the source of Life, and I wither and pale . . .

(Little pause.)

MICHL

Your grandfather was a disciple of the Baal Shem Tov, Rebbe, your father was a tzaddik, and there are generations behind them of wise men and saints, and these all stand behind you, Rabbi Azriel, they guard and fortify you, as they always have. Your holy father Ishtele saw the Prophet Elijah, three times. When Mayer Ber your uncle recited the Sh'ma Yisroel he would rise to the ceiling of the shul and sometimes he floated up to Heaven, and the great Velvele your blessed grandfather brought the dead to life.

RABBI AZRIEL

Do you know, Michl, how my grandfather drove out dybbuks?

He'd bellow, "HAAAAAAA!" No words or prayers or minyans. He'd simply yell at a dybbuk and the dybbuk went. "HAAAAAAAAA!"
Of course the rabbis were all much mightier back then.
(He looks up to Heaven for a moment, and then says to Shimshin and Michl) We must prepare ourselves. Go inside. I'll join you in a moment.

(Shimshin and Michl withdraw.)

RABBI AZRIEL
(To the air) Holy Velvele, you stand behind this chair and grip my shoulders! You have been dead sixty-seven years; in that time I only grow weaker, and the world grows wickeder. But you in Paradise have grown stronger, and I ask you to accompany me now. In Lublin, in Zlotchov, pogroms. The people talk idly of traveling and scientific marvels and don't pray. I'm older than my years, I don't sleep at night. Under my robe, my knees knock together in fear sometimes. *(Softly)* And sometimes, Grandfather, I do not entirely trust God. *(To the Scribe)* Don't write that down.

Act Four

❧

SCENE 1

An hour later. The same room as Act Three. Where the broad Sabbath dining table stood there is a now a smaller table, behind which are Rabbi Azriel's armchair flanked by three smaller chairs. Rabbi Azriel and the two other Rabbinical Judges are seated in the armchair and two of the smaller chairs, in prayer shawls and phylacteries. Rabbi Shimshin, similarly attired, is standing at one end of the table. Michl stands in attendance, the Scribe is writing furiously. In one corner a curtain is hanging. The men are praying together in Hebrew. The sounds of prayers continue to come from the adjoining rooms. Azriel says:

RABBI AZRIEL

Ohmayn.

(He stands and, holding a long cane, he walks to the curtain. Drawing from left to right Azriel makes a circle on the floor with his cane, saying:)

RABBI AZRIEL

We summon Nissin ben Rivka now to appear before the Rabbinical Court. Nissin I will command you to appear within this circle behind this curtain we have hung for you, for your modesty and for our protection; you may not leave it. Sender!

SENDER

Yes Rabbi?

RABBI AZRIEL

We have summoned the righteous dead man Nissin. Will you accept our judgment?

SENDER

I will accept it.

RABBI AZRIEL

And comply with its every demand?

SENDER

I'll do what I am told.

RABBI AZRIEL

Good. Go stand over there.

SENDER

I've thought through the night, Rabbi, I didn't sleep, and I remember something, a pact I made with Nissin, which I have broken but . . .

RABBI AZRIEL

(Clapping his hands with impatient anger!) Sender! Sender! Sender! I am not your teacher and you are not my pupil anymore! Now go stand where I tell you. Await the plaintiff and the presentation of his complaint.

SENDER

(As he goes to the spot the Rabbi had indicated) But I broke it in genuine ignorance, and this is perhaps . . .

RABBI AZRIEL

Ssssshhhhhh!

(Everyone is silent.)

RABBI AZRIEL

A being from the True World is about to enter this room, to our world, the world of Illusion, to demand of us that we settle his grievance against this man through strict application of the laws of the Torah, which as this trial proves governs not only the world but all the universe.

(Pause)

The trial will be watched by the heavens, by their entire populations; wheels and dominions, the zazahot and the ten sefirot; one of their citizens has come to us for Justice. We are in danger, therefore, for no deviation from the law is permitted, and the censure is destruction. And so as all judges must, we sit in the awful majesty of the law, full of fear.

THE FIRST RABBINICAL JUDGE

The plaintiff is here, Rabbi. I've grown cold . . .

THE SECOND RABBINICAL JUDGE

And I smell earth, and ash. I taste metal on my tongue.

THE SCRIBE

(Chanting softly in Hebrew as he writes) N'vakeysh et nitzotzot hanefesh matzitey m'orey ha'eysh. N'haleyl et nishmat kol chay unvareych al miney b'samim.

RABBI SHIMSHIN

(Over the above) I believe Nissin has come.

RABBI AZRIEL

Righteous dead man, Nissin ben Rivka, do you agree to stay within the circle the Rabbinical Court has prepared for you? And will you obey our command and tell the Rabbinical Court your complaint against Sender ben Henya?

(A terrifying pause, and silence; all listen, petrified.)

THE FIRST RABBINICAL JUDGE
I hear a chanting, keening voice without words.

THE SECOND RABBINICAL JUDGE
Before my eyes I see an ancient hand scribing letters, but I hear
nothing!

THE SCRIBE
(In a huge voice) N'VAREYCH ET EYN HACHAYIM,
M'KOR HAVCHANAH! NIZKEH NA L'HAVIN
ULHASKIL, LISHOMO'A, LIMOD UL'LAMEYD, LISH-
MOR V'LA'ASOT ULKAYEYM DIVREY TORAH B'A-
HAVAH.

RABBI SHIMSHIN
(To Sender) Sender ben Henya. The righteous dead man Nissin
ben Rivka claims the following against you: You were both
young men in this yeshiva years ago, you were true friends;
once during the Days of Awe, when all oaths are especially
sacrosanct, you vowed that your love for one another and the
union of your souls would one day become flesh. When the
women you married had conceived, if the Almighty would
make one bear a daughter and one bear a son, these your children would become husband and wife. You vowed this to each
other, you swore before . . .

SENDER
We did, I suppose, we . . . Yes, but it was terribly long ago and
then he . . .

RABBI SHIMSHIN
The righteous dead man claims that after he had left Miropol
and traveled to a remote shtetl, his wife had a son and yours
had a daughter.

SENDER

I had a daughter but I didn't know anything more from him, he . . .

RABBI SHIMSHIN

It was soon after his son was born that Nissin the righteous man died.

SENDER

NISSIN! I never knew you had a boy, I . . . .

THE SCRIBE

(Loud, keening) HEYEYH ASHER TIHYEH, VEHEYEYH BARUCH BA'ASHER TIHYEH!

RABBI SHIMSHIN

AND I LEARNED . . . THAT MY SON . . . HAD A BLESSED SOUL . . . EXALTED, HE . . . ROSE LIKE A FALCON IN THE MOUNTAINS, HIGHER, HIGHER, TOUCHING CLOUDS, I WAS . . . VERY PROUD.

(Pause)

But my boy . . . wandered . . . town to town, crossing borders, for his soul . . . KNEW, IT WAS SEEKING! WHAT YOU AND I HAD VOWED! HIS . . . Beloved. Intended.

(Pause)

And he found her at your house, Sender, at your table.

(Little pause)

But Nissin's son was a poor student and you Sender, you are a rich man. So you ignored your daughter's destined bridegroom, you searched elsewhere for your son-in-law . . . This horror has come . . . AND MORE WILL COME . . . Because you are a dishonest! Desperate! Greedy Man! MY SON MEANWHILE . . . BURNED!

He wandered . . . again but now . . . BLIND, in despair! The new paths he sought led to dark places, AND I . . . COULD NOT WARN HIM! Till the boy fell prey to the Sitra-Achra and its light-devouring false beauty, to the demons that dragged him untimely from the world.

(Little pause)
And now: Nissin's son has become a dybbuk min ha-hizonim, and his soul has stolen into the body of his beloved.

(Little pause)
Nissin ben Rivka claims before this Court: His son is dead, his wife dead too, and now his own name is not remembered by anyone, he has no grandchildren now nor ever will, and no one says Kaddish for Nissin ben Rivka. His light, his best loved child, has died now for all eternity. He asks of the Court this judgment of Sender ben Henya: Sender has spilled the blood of Nissin's son, and his son's children, and theirs, and theirs, until the End of Days.

(Pause. Sender weeps.)

RABBI AZRIEL
Sender ben Henya, you've heard the charges the righteous dead man has brought. How do you answer?

SENDER
I can barely speak.
(Little pause)
Nissin my old friend, I can't justify this terrible wrong or undo the evil that's been done already, but it was a sin committed ignorantly, not because I bore anyone malice, you least of all. Nissin you moved away after that Yom Kippur when we made our vows, and I didn't know you'd had a son. I never heard from you again. Years passed before I learned you'd died.

RABBI AZRIEL
Did you send after him? Try to learn where he'd gone, investigate?

SENDER
Years passed. Day by day, I simply forgot.

(Little pause.)

RABBI SHIMSHIN

Nissin ben Rivka would like to know—Sender: Why you never asked his son, who was a visitor at your table many times, what his name was or what town he was from?

SENDER

I don't . . . that was a long time ago, too, I can't remember now; don't suspect my motives, Nissin, you were the bridegroom's father, it was your job to approach me and anyway, look at how I tried to keep her unmarried, I was impossible with the marriage terms, I kept three suitors away from her because in my heart I knew someone would come for her, your son, but . . . Finally, this last suitor, his family's powerful and compliant and . . .

RABBI SHIMSHIN

I . . . SUSPECT your motives, and your heart, SENDER . . . because in the heart within the heart within you knew who this boy was . . . who resembled his father so strongly . . . YOU DID NOT ASK WHO HIS FATHER WAS BECAUSE YOU DIDN'T WANT TO KNOW.
To make your daughter rich and comfortable, you exiled his son to a demon-haunted abyss.

(Pause.)

RABBI AZRIEL

We will render our decision now.

(The Rabbis confer while Sender covers his face, weeping quietly.)

RABBI AZRIEL

The Rabbinical Court, its power descending from God, having listened to both parties, has decided this: Something that has not been created cannot be bound up in an oath, and since we do not know if conception had taken place in either wife when the vows were made, it cannot be determined if the vows were binding here on earth. Nevertheless, the heavens must have accepted these vows, for Nissin's son knew of the promise in his heart, and sought his bride; and furthermore great tragedy has resulted from Sender's failure to keep honor with his friend. It is thus the judgment of the Rabbinical Court that, since the absolute truth is caught halfway between this world and the next, Sender must give half of all he has to the poor; not a kopek less than half. And for the rest of his life Sender is to burn yahrzeit candles and recite the mourner's Kaddish each year for Nissin ben Rivka and for Nissin's son. As if these dead were of his own family.

(Little pause)

The Rabbinical Court asks the righteous dead man Nissin ben Rivka to forgive Sender completely and for all eternity, and at the same time to use his paternal authority to command his son to leave the body of Sender's daughter Leah; for if he doesn't he will kill a living branch of the people Israel. Help us, Nissin, and the Almighty will then show his vast grace to Nissin, and to his homeless son.

THE MESSENGER

AMEN!

RABBI AZRIEL

Nissin ben Rivka, have you heard the judgment of this Court and do you accept it?

(A fearful pause)

Do you accept our judgment?

(A fearful pause)

I, Azriel, son of Ishtele son of Velvele command you Righteous dead man Nissin ben Rivka to answer me!

(Silence)

Sender ben Henya, have you heard the judgment of this Court and do you accept it?

SENDER

I . . . I accept. Yes, but he . . . .

RABBI AZRIEL

Righteous dead man Nissin ben Rivka, the litigation is ended now between you and Sender ben Henya. You must return to your realm, the True World, and we enjoin you to forebear hurting any living creature as you leave. Michl! Remove the curtain, clear a space in the room, and send for water! And tell the minyan to prepare itself!

(Michl goes to the door, opens it, says something to a servant outside, and then removes the curtain. Rabbi Azriel draws the circle with his cane again, but this time right to left, and a servant enters with water and a pitcher. Everyone washes their hands as the other three Rabbis talk in whispers:)

RABBI SHIMSHIN

The dead man didn't forgive Sender.

THE FIRST RABBINICAL JUDGE

I know. What can that mean?

THE SECOND RABBINICAL JUDGE

And the dead man didn't say he accepted the judgment.

RABBI SHIMSHIN

Or say Amen to Rebbe Azriel's conclusion. Nissin's hatred must be very hot and inextinguishable. I think something terrible is coming.

THE FIRST RABBINICAL JUDGE

Rabbi Azriel is frightened, his hands shake.

THE SECOND RABBINICAL JUDGE

This is an ill-omened Court, and my business here is through.

(The First and Second Rabbinical Judges leave furtively.)

RABBI AZRIEL

(To Sender) Is the bridegroom here yet?

A Dybbuk

SENDER

I haven't heard their carriage, Rebbe.

RABBI AZRIEL

Go send another rider to hasten them on their way, what's keeping them? See that the preparations are made for the wedding in the shul, a canopy, musicians, tell them to be ready to play loudly, and bring in the bride. She's been dressed in her bridal gown?

(Sender nods.)

RABBI AZRIEL

Go! Go!
(Removing his prayer shawl and phylacteries) Lord of Creation, King of the Universe, do You amuse Yourself? At my expense? Very well, laugh, Blessed name! But I swear before you I will undo this pact, even if it was pledged at the foot of Your Throne, I will tear these two asunder, it is Unholy! If I am wrong, break me like a bottle, but I will work this wonder in Your Name!

(Sender and Fradde lead Leah in. She is dressed again in her wedding gown, with a black cloak over that. She is seated on the sofa. Shimshin stands next to Azriel.)

RABBI AZRIEL

Dybbuk! In the name of the Chief Rabbi of Miropol, in the names of a holy minyan of Jews, in the name of the august Sanhedrin in Jerusalem, I, Azriel ben Hadas, command you a final time: Leave the body of this girl!

THE DYBBUK

I CANNOT! I WILL NEVER LEAVE!

RABBI AZRIEL

Michl, open the inner doors.

(Michl does so, and fourteen men enter in white robes, each carrying either a ram's horn or black candle.)

RABBI AZRIEL

Open the Ark. Remove the Torahs.

(Michl opens the Ark and removes seven scrolls, which are handed to seven of the minyan.)

RABBI AZRIEL

Wicked and obdurate spirit, ru'ah tezazit, Dybbuk me-ru'ah ra'ah, having defied my decree and my authority, I must now call Metatron and the Kerubim, Raphael, Michael, Gabriel and Sandalphon, the mightiest of the angels, all praises be, to marshall the spirits of the upper air to pry you loose from this living child. Blow the horns! TEKIAH!

(The men blow their horns, "TEKIAH!"
Leah screams, leaps up; Sender and Fradde try to hold her but she pushes them away, and then falls and writhes on the ground.)

THE DYBBUK

LEAVE ME! LEAVE ME! DON'T PULL ME AWAY! I DON'T WANT TO GO! I CAN'T! I CAN'T!

RABBI AZRIEL

Since you have not submitted to the upper air, I next call on the Shedim Yehuda'im, demons submissive to the Almighty Torah, demons of the middle air, caught between worlds, between good and evil, I place you under their savage authority, and let their iron claws tear you away! Blow the horns. SHVORIM!

(Again the horns blast, "SHVORIM!"
Leah writhes and the Dybbuk shouts, but with waning strength:)

THE DYBBUK

OH Most High, Holy King, all the powers of creation have turned against me! Demons and angels and a host of righteous souls, souls, and my father is with them, and they command me to go, their voices are thunder, ice and searing heat, but I defy you all! Kill me if you want me gone but while I have strength I WILL NOT LET GO!

RABBI AZRIEL
(To himself, shaken) Something powerful is helping him!

(Pause. Then the Rabbi says to Michl, quietly:)

RABBI AZRIEL
Michl, put the Torahs back in the Ark.

(Michl and the other men do this.)

RABBI AZRIEL
Shroud the Ark in black.

(A black cloth is placed over the Ark.)

RABBI AZRIEL
Now the candles must be lit.

(As the black candles are lit Michl helps Rabbi Azriel and Rabbi Shimshin into white robes.
There is a hush in the room and Rabbi Azriel stands over the girl, raising his arm and intoning in a terrifying voice:)

RABBI AZRIEL
God Almighty, rise up from your Throne, fly as a Vulture that hastens to devour, terrible and dreadful, a leopard and a wolf, the foaming of mighty waters, whose great day is near, whose day of waste and desolation is near, Lord of the Saltpits, of the breeding-place of nettles, in the name of the Patriarchs, in the name of Matriarchs, of the martyred and the slain, in the name of the blood of the God of Wrath and Vengeance, I, Azriel ben Hadas, break every thread that binds you, spirit of the dybbukim, to the world of the living and to the body of the daughter of Channa! GO!

THE DYBBUK

(Shrieking) GOD!

RABBI AZRIEL

And from the community and the people Israel, I anathematize and exile you! TERUAH!

THE MESSENGER

The spark shatters the vessel, and dissolves in the flame.

THE DYBBUK

I cannot . . . hold . . . I cannot hold on . . .

(The men blast "TERUAH" on the rams' horns. The Rabbi holds his hand up for silence.)

RABBI AZRIEL

Dybbuk, are you slipping away?

THE DYBBUK

(Very weak) I . . . I am dying, Rebbe.

RABBI AZRIEL

Then with all my power I rescind your anathema.
(To Michl and the other men) Put out all the candles and tear down the shroud. Hide the rams' horns. And all of you in the minyan must leave. Michl take them out. Immediately.

(They obey the Rabbi's instructions. The men of the quorum, including the Messenger, and Michl as well, leave the room.)

RABBI AZRIEL

God of Mercy and Goodness, forgive this homeless and tormented soul, take him in Your loving hands and heal his injuries, strike his sins from the Book of Life, and for his early life of piety and good works and great learning, for all that he has suffered, and for the righteousness of his ancestors, Lord of the Universe who alone forgives and judges, and whose compassion is infinite, save him from demons and prepare a room for his rest in Your palace of splendors. Amen.

THE MESSENGER

Amen!

(Leah shudders violently.)

THE DYBBUK

Say Kaddish for me, I am dying.

RABBI AZRIEL

Sender!

SENDER

Yisgadal ve-yiskadash shmey rabo b'olma di b'ra chirusey . . . magnified and Sanctified be His Great Name throughout the World that He has created according to his Will. May He establish His kingdom in your lifetime and in your days, and in the lifetime of all the House of Israel, soon, with speed. And say Amen.

(A clock strikes twelve. Leah jumps to her feet, looking about, terror-stricken, and screams. And then she falls to the floor, unconscious.)

RABBI AZRIEL

Now we must move with haste. Take the bride to the canopy! Surely the others have finally . . .

(Michl runs in, frightened.)

MICHL

Rabbi, you must come, the bridegroom and his family are on the outskirts of the town, their carriage lost its wheels, their mules have died, the riders we sent after them, their horses went wild and charged off into the night, and on the outskirts of town all the cocks have started crowing, at midnight, the bridegroom has fainted, they've carried him on foot but they're

suddenly so stricken with terror they cannot take another step!
You must come now!

RABBI AZRIEL

Sender! This is the golden destiny your negotiations have
bought you!

THE SCRIBE

Rabbi! I turned to a new page in your record book, and look!
It's already filled! It was pure, unwritten-upon a moment ago,
and . . .

(Little pause. The Rabbi looks at the book the Scribe's holding.)

RABBI AZRIEL

Read.

THE SCRIBE

(Reading:)

Rabbi, only turn the page:
the wonders of the coming age
will dwarf your shtetl magic so—
dybbuks, golems, all you know,
your writings and the words you say,
like oven ashes, swept away.
At some not-very-distant date
the martyred dead accumulate;
books of history will contain
mountain-piles of the slain.

*(The Rabbi and the Messenger look at one another. The Rabbi nods
his head.)*

RABBI AZRIEL

What must be will be.
(To Fradde) Woman, to your loving care I entrust this bride.

A Dybbuk

(He draws a circle, right to left, around Fradde and Leah.)

Sender and Michl you will come with me.
(To the Scribe) Write nothing further of the events of this night.
Take what you have written, wrap it in a shroud, go to the river
and drown this Book.

*(The Rabbi, the Scribe, Sender and Michl exit, leaving Fradde and
Leah alone.)*

LEAH
(Waking up) Who's here . . . ? Oh Fradde. Fradde I'm so tired,
and horribly cold; cradle me. Every limb is heavy . . .

(Fradde cradles Leah.)

FRADDE
You shouldn't feel heavy now, my darling one, my own, let the
rat feel heavy, let the cat feel heavy, you should feel like a
goosedown feather, the breath of an infant, a snowflake, the
wind in the wings of the angels . . .

LEAH
(Shuddering) Fradde I'm frightened, I hear feet drumming the
ground, they're dancing around the grave of the Martyred
Couple, they're dancing for the dead bride and her groom.

FRADDE
Don't shiver, darling, sixty Maccabees with bronze swords and
shields surround us, the Matriarchs too, and no evil can reach
us here . . .

(She begins to sing softly:)

Soon to the canopy you will be led,
Your mother arrives from the World of the dead,
And she comes to your wedding in silver and gold,
She offers her hands for the angels to hold.

Oh Channala's daughter's a glorious bride.
Does Channala glitter with gold or with pride?
Then Channa your mother says, bursting with joy,
"My Leah is marrying a wonderful boy."
But suddenly, Channala, why do you sigh,
And why does your heart break, and why do you cry?
"Strangers are leading the bridal parade
While I stand, unseen, alone and afraid.
The living are dancing with those that they see,
And only the dead will be dancing with me."
And the daughter of Channa is married that day
To the bridegroom who's waiting to dance her away.
But
See the klezmorim, they sing and they play,
And all through the dancing, the spirits will stray,
Among them, Eliahu, he dances and sings
And silver and gold are the blessings he brings.
And shekels slop over the Prophet's gold cup,
And the living and dead rush to gobble them up . . .
Soon to the canopy you will be lead;
Your mother arrives from the world of the dead.
Amen, Amen . . .

(Fradde lies back and quickly falls asleep; Leah too is drowsing, when she hears a loud sigh and sits up.)

LEAH

Who sighed so brokenly?

CHONEN'S VOICE

I did.

LEAH

I can't see you.

CHONEN'S VOICE
They've torn us apart, and around you there's a magic circle.

LEAH

Your voice is like a violin on a summer's night, playing a melody I remember . . . Who are you?

CHONEN'S VOICE

I've forgotten. I can remember only if you remember me . . .

LEAH

I do. I remember. On summer nights I would open the window in my room, and there was always a low bright star that burned brave and alone, it made me cry with loneliness. And then someone in my dreams came at night. And he was that horizon light. Was that you?

CHONEN'S VOICE

Yes.

LEAH

I remember. You had delicate hair and sad eyes; pale, mild hands with long, slender fingers, and every night belonged to you, and every day you haunted me . . .
(Little pause)
Why did you leave me again?

CHONEN'S VOICE

Every wall they placed between us I knocked down, I conquered death, but they were too many, and too strong; and when they'd trampled out my flame in you, I left your body so that I might come to your soul.

LEAH

Come to me my bridegroom, enter my heart, let me bear you there, my dead man, till in dreams at night I can deliver you, in dreams at night we can cradle the children we will never have . . .

(A wedding march is heard outside.)

LEAH

They're bringing the stranger in, they want me to marry him.
Come to me my bridegroom.

CHONEN'S VOICE

I left your body to return to your soul.

(Wearing white for his wedding, Chonen appears.)

LEAH

The circle's broken! I am coming to you! I'm so afraid!

CHONEN

Please, come to me.

LEAH

I am!

*(As the wedding march grows stronger, Leah removes her black
cloak and approaches the bridegroom. The two become one.
The Messenger enters. Rabbi Azriel follows, the others behind him.
Azriel stops them by the door.)*

LEAH

(In a faraway voice) He is light and I am flame and we join into
Holy fire and rise, and rise, and rise . . .

*(Chonen lowers Leah's lifeless body to the floor. He takes a flame
from her breast, and stands apart, in a golden light, unseen,
waiting . . .*
The others gather around Leah's body.)

RABBI AZRIEL

It is too late.

SENDER

Leah . . .

THE MESSENGER

Boruch dayan ho-emes.

(The Rabbi looks at the Messenger.)

RABBI AZRIEL

(Softly) It doesn't matter. Tell Him that. The more cause He gives to doubt Him. Tell Him that. The deeper delves faith. Though His love become only abrasion, derision, excoriation, tell Him, I cling. We cling. He made us, He can never shake us off. We will always find Him out. Promise Him that. We will always find Him, no matter how few there are, tell Him we will find Him. To deliver our complaint.

THE MESSENGER

I accept the commission.

RABBI AZRIEL

Sender, tip the messenger.

SENDER

My daughter.

(Sender gives the Messenger a gold coin.)

RABBI AZRIEL

Travel swiftly.

THE MESSENGER

Blessed be the true judge. May they rest in Paradise.

(The lights die. Leah rises and joins Chonen in his golden light; they dance until darkness overwhelms the stage. In darkness we hear the lone voice again:)

A LONE VOICE, CHANTING

Why did the soul,
Oh tell me this,

Tumble from Heaven
To the Great Abyss?
The most profound descents contain
Ascensions to the heights again . . .

END OF PLAY

Afterword
by Harold Bloom

I suspect that Tony Kushner's *Angels in America*, a generation from now, will have lost much of its political aura, and will seem essentially a religious drama, heterodox, and part of the long history of Jewish Gnosticism. Roy Cohn, in Kushner's vision of him, has a negative exuberance akin to Nathaniel West's Shrike in *Miss Lonelyhearts*. Wonderfully persuasive throughout, and the glory of *Angels in America*, Cohn is most memorable in the afterlife, where he takes as his client, Yahweh, who faces an angelic lawsuit for desertion. Shouting demoniac pride in his own legal (and extra-legal) skills, Cohn affirms both absolute confidence in winning the case and an accurate conviction as to Yahweh's guilt. Cohn's audacity culminates the joyous spirituality of Kushner's two-part play, always more effective in its negations than in its social affirmations, poignantly wistful as they can be.

Phantasmagoria is an immensely difficult dramatic mode, unless you are the Shakespeare of *Macbeth*. Kushner has an authentic gift for fantasy; it is not surprising that he would compose *A Dybbuk*, and may go on to *A Golem*. His "dramatic legend" purports to be an adaptation of Ansky's Yiddish warhorse, aided by Neugroschel's translation of the original. As a playgoer with memories of the Yiddish theatre of half a century ago, I am charmed by the freedom of the "adaptation," which replaces a normative work by a thoroughly Gnostic play, Kushner's own. The first lines recall Nathan of Gaza, Shabbatei Zevi's prophet, whose myth of divine degradation was summarized by Gershom Scholem as "redemption through sin," the imaginative doctrine of Kushner's Chonen the Kabbalist, who in death becomes the Dybbuk inhabiting his beloved, Leah. As in *Angels in America*, all of us have tumbled from Heaven to the Great Abyss, particularized by Kushner (rather wickedly) as Ronald Reagan's America.

Kabbalistically, there is no written Torah, as Chonen implies, but only "infinite combinations," including his interpretation that from his Leah one can spell "Not God." Eloquently, Chonen dismisses the Talmud as "earth above and earth below," and affirms Kabbalah where "eyes within eyes have opened wide." I hear in Chonen a wiser Kushner, who knows the limitations of Brechtian theatrical politics: "Purify a whole generation and the next generation appears unrepentant." Redemption comes not from banishing sin, but by making sin holy, the gesture of Leah when she passionately kisses the Torah, palpable surrogate for Chonen. Literally starving himself to death, for love of Leah, Chonen envisages a purely aesthetic Third Temple, and blasphemes God's name by whispering its unsayable form to the ambiguous Messenger, whose relation to the Angelic world is clarified at the end. Kushner is a long way beyond the normative Blessing of "more life" when he has Chonen triumph by dying: "Wherever she is I will be rekindled." A mutual love-death blasphemes the Blessing, or ought to, but not in Kushner's *A Dybbuk*. "The dead should not be excluded from any celebration," the Messenger remarks, which suggests many traditions, but not quite the normative one (until it fused with Lurianic Kabbalah in Hasidism).

Kushner (politics aside) shrewdly is writing his own New Kabbalah, which was also Kafka's enigmatic ambition. Leah, lamenting Chonen, is more than complicit when his spirit possesses her. Perhaps one could say that this possession, disaster in Ansky, is welcomed by Kushner in ways that surpass a dramatist's needs. When Rabbi Azriel cites Torah that the dead may not dwell among the living, and the Dybbuk cries out: "I never died!" Kushner's own spirit divides. Kushner's Dybbuk says: "I never died!" because the Gnostic God, exiled from all the worlds, is not responsible for the catastrophe of the Creation-Fall, worshiped by the Hasidism even though it is the botched effort of a demiurge whom they wrongly identify as Yahweh. The Gnostic spark, never born, can never die, and the union of Leah and Chonen, blasphemy to Rabbi Azriel, has a status in Kushner less fearful than it did in Ansky. It is difficult not to hear the irony when Azriel surmises that Leah suffers Chonen's possession: "simply so that we may turn her sufferings into a text—for others to study in the ages to come."

The Messenger is Kushner's only character for whom everything is not overdetermined, since both the normative Hasidism and the Kabbalist Chonen suffer from Jewish memory, in which everything has happened already, and all meaning is in the past. Part of the drama's strength is its alternation of Chonen and the Messenger as Kushner's near-surrogates, which suggests the ongoing odyssey of the playwright's still-unfolding spirituality. The Messenger's fatalism establishes him as another of Kushner's Angels, badly needed in a play where the holy Azriel sums up the normative vision: "The room is cold, the world is cold, its variety is deceptive, there's not so much to see." This recalls Kafka's mordant observation that Abraham mistook a handful of dust for the uniformity of the world. Kafka grimly might have appreciated Azriel's observation: "Jews have merely tumbled from the pages of books."

Azriel represents a waning tradition; his God is elusive, and the rabbi is not capable of totally defeating a Dybbuk as knowing as Chonen. Not to trust God is to lose trust in the Covenant, and Azriel does "not entirely trust God." Since the sin of the poor Sender, Leah's father, is mostly forgetfulness, compounded by greed, it is a violent shock when the Rabbinical Court's judgment receives no response from Nissin, the righteous dead man who was Chonen's father. Azriel chillingly wonders if God is amusing himself at the rabbi's expense, and presses on in the normatively holy but pragmatically terrible quest to expel Chonen from Leah. "The spark shatters the vessel, and dissolves in the flame" is the Messenger's response, as he recalls the initial Breaking of the Vessels of the Creation-Fall. Kushner associates this with the Holocaust the major "wonder of the coming age."

Unable to fuse as bodies, Leah and Chonen unite as souls, which completes the disaster of the exorcism, clearly symbolic for Kushner of the dying of normative tradition. We are close to a darker version of *Perestroika* when Azriel and the Messenger conclude the play with a last confrontation, where it is difficult even for Azriel not to identify God as deserter or exile: "We will always find Him out. Promise Him that. We will always find Him, no matter how few there are, tell Him we will find Him. To deliver our complaint."

The Messenger accepts the commission, and so the complaint will be heard, but God will be acquitted, since He has the cunning to have retained Roy Cohn as his attorney. Kushner will have to create an Angel capable of besting Roy Cohn if this latest of New Kabbalahs indeed is to manage: "ascensions to the heights again."

THE
DYBBUK
MELODY

And Other Themes and Variations

Translations from Yiddish by

Joachim Neugroschel

JOACHIM NEUGROSCHEL WOULD LIKE TO THANK

MORDKHE SCHAECHTER, SHULEM MALIK

AND MATTI MEGGED

FOR THEIR HELP.

Introduction

❧

Like many other Yiddish authors, S. Ansky (1863–1920) wrote not only realistic but also supernatural stories, for which he drew on the mystical tales handed down in Chasidic communities. Some of this material was derived from the Talmud and some from the Cabala, though heavily simplified and popularized; indeed, the hermetic lore and arcane erudition of the medieval Cabalists was turned upside down by Chasidism, which preaches plain and direct understanding of religion—especially by the uneducated. A crucial factor in Chasidic life is the *tsáddik* (or *rébbe* or *guter-yíd*), the "guru" of a sect: and Chasidic literature, both oral and written, is replete with paeans to and legends about these leaders.

A background for the world of *A Dybbuk* can be partly found in the narratives translated here. In addition to some of Ansky's own supernatural pieces, we are including some of the folktales he collected in 1912–1914, when his ethnographic expedition visited Jewish communities throughout Eastern Europe, gathering songs and stories, rituals and superstitions. In order to tie them together, the selection of these folktales concentrates on stories about music. And, to add a romantic touch, we have also added an erotic fantasy by Dovid-Ber Horovitz (1895–1942), who so sensually depicted Chasidism against the pantheistic backdrop of the Carpathian landscape.

Yielding to modernism, industrialism, and technology,

disrupted by pogroms, economic chaos, and mass emigration, Jewish life in Eastern Europe went through drastic transformations. World War I, the Russian Revolution, and the collapse of both the tsarist and the Austro-Hungarian empires brought a complete restructuring. The world depicted in Ansky's *Dybbuk* had fairly vanished when he died in 1920, just before the premiere of his play in Warsaw. Two decades later, the German occupation wiped out most of Ashkenazi civilization.

The Dybbuk Melody

(Folktale)

The town cantor of Vishnevitz, a Chasid who was a follower of Rabbi Dúvidl of Tálne, was getting on in years, and his voice was no longer what it should have been. A large number of worshipers were dissatisfied and felt it was time to get a new cantor. But his fellow Chasidim wouldn't hear of it, and so for a while the town was in the grips of a quiet feud.

Now one day the cantor became extremely hoarse, and since his hoarseness wouldn't go away, many of the Chasidim finally agreed that he ought to be replaced.

As is customary among Jews, they came to terms with the old cantor, who had no choice but to consent. And so a young successor was hired. The new cantor was an excellent musician and a God-fearing Jew. All the townsfolk were delighted by the sweetness and beauty of his voice, and they greatly admired him for his piety and other fine virtues.

The old cantor, who had been removed from office, could not get over his downfall. He regarded the new cantor as an arch-enemy whom he envied and hated. With the approach of the Days of Awe, his resentment grew so strong that he became fatally ill, and on the eve of Rosh-ha-Shonah (New Year's) he was brought to his eternal rest.

Everyone was saddened by his death, and quite a few of

his former opponents were sick at heart, feeling that they had helped to cause his premature death. The new cantor, that pious young man, was likewise in mortal anguish, and he walked about careworn and shattered, as if he were wandering through the World of Chaos. He believed he shared the responsibility for the old cantor's distress, which may have ended his life so quickly.

And then, something terrible happened to the new cantor. It was the first day of Rosh-ha-Shonah. That morning he was supposed to sing his own version of the prayer: "Here I am, poor in deeds," which cantors have been singing since the Middle Ages. But even though he had so carefully rehearsed it with the choir, he suddenly broke off in confusion—his mind was a blank. He closed his eyes, wracked his memory, but it was no use, he couldn't remember a single note. All at once, the ghost of the dead cantor hovered before him, and the music came pouring from the new cantor's throat—but not the melody that he had practiced. It was the one that the old cantor had sung for many years. The worshipers instantly recognized the old cantor's voice and even his version.

The new cantor collapsed. The worshipers clustered around him and tried to carry him out of the synagogue. But with extraordinary strength he tore himself out of their hands and dashed over to the lectern, where the hoarse voice of the old cantor came venomously pouring from the new cantor's throat: "I am still the cantor of this town! This is my lectern, and I will sing my own version and my own melody!"

The young cantor fainted and was carried home, and one of the householders led the congregation in prayer.

Shortly after Rosh-ha-Shonah, the young cantor was taken to see Rabbi Dúvidl in Tálne. The rabbi led the cantor into his private study and, after locking the door, ordered him to sing his version of the prayer. But all that emerged was the hoarse voice of the dead cantor.

This infuriated Rabbi Dúvidl, and he angrily snapped: "A pious melody should be sweet and pleasant, and prayer must be blissful, especially during the dreadful time of the Days of Awe." Then he went on in Hebrew: "Let it be Thy will before

Thee, fearful God, that my voice shall not be interrupted and my voice shall not become hoarse and my voice shall grow stronger and stronger like the loud, clear blast of the Shofar." Next, in Yiddish, he said: "The cantor's voice must be able to move the Lord of the Universe. And in order to move Him, the voice must be finer and more beautiful than yours. Go back to your rest and let your successor use his own sweet and beautiful voice to lead the prayers, so that he may bring salvation to his community of Jews!"

A long, faint weeping could be heard. Rabbi Dúvidl began speaking again, and his words were no longer angry now but calm and soft. He said, first in Hebrew, then in Yiddish: "You two cantors, both the old one and the young one, should prick up your ears and hear me out as I sing my own version of the prayer. Both of you, listen closely and memorize the melody for your own good."

And in a pure voice Rabbi Dúvidl began to sing his own version, a new melody. And the more he sang, the stronger his voice became, soaring higher and higher in great heartfelt bliss and sacred ecstasy. When Rabbi Dúvidl was done, he raised his moist eyes, stretched out his hands, and said very tenderly: "Now, holy dead man, go back to your rest immediately. This melody will open all gates for you and undo all bolts. Your soul will receive its full salvation, and I promise you that you will be privileged to sing this melody in front of the righteous in Paradise!"

Rabbi Dúvidl then went over to the young cantor and, peering deep into his eyes, he embraced him and said: "Now let's both of us try to sing my melody together. The old cantor is gone. He will never appear at your lectern again!"

And Rabbi Dúvidl once more launched into his own melody. The young cantor sang along, for he had regained his own young, clear voice, which sounded purer and more mellow than ever.

And for years and years, Rabbi Dúvidl's Chasidim sang that melody, which became known as the "Dybbuk Melody."

A Human Life

S. Ansky

(1910)

❧

When a human being is about to be created, God Praised Be He, signals to the angel named Laila (Night), and says to him: "Know that at this very moment a person is being created from a certain drop, so please bring that drop to my Throne of Glory."

And the angel carries out the Almighty's order and brings the drop to the threshold of the Throne of Glory. The Almighty then decrees whether the new human being will be male or female, weak or strong, rich or poor, beautiful or ugly. However God does not determine whether this person will be good or bad, righteous or wicked.

And the Holy Blessed Be He signals to the angel in charge of souls and says: "Fly to the Garden of Eden, go to the great storehouse, and bring me such and such a soul with such and such an appearance." For all the souls that have already been created since the Six Days of Creation and have to be created until the end of time are created for the sake of man.

And the angel who is the custodian of souls flies to the great storehouse, brings back the assigned soul, and places it at the threshold to the Throne of Glory. And the Almighty says: "Soul! Go into that drop, penetrate all its six hundred sixty-six limbs, and let it be your dwelling place until the end of this person's life."

And the soul bows and prostrates itself before the Almighty and opens its lips and tremblingly implores God: "Lord of All Worlds, I am very content with the world I've been living in since You created me. And if this is Your almighty will, do not put me into an unworthy drop, for I am pure and holy."

And the Almighty answers the soul: "The drop I'm putting you in is also a world, a holy and limitless world. And this new world is more suitable for you than the world you've been living in. For when you were created you were destined only for this drop."

And the soul weeps, and its weeping can be heard from one end of the universe to the other. And its weeping is joined by the weeping of all the other souls and also the angels and the seraphim. But the Almighty does not listen to their weeping and He forces the soul into the drop.

Then he summons the angel Laila and orders him to place the drop in the innards of the mother. And at that moment the drop becomes a fetus, a child in the mother's innards.

The Almighty provides the newly created fetus with two guardian angels, a bright one and a dark one.

Every morning, the bright angel takes the fetus and carries it to the Garden of Eden and points to the righteous, who sit in a vast aura with crowns on their heads and are imbued with the lustrous beauty of the Shekhina, the Divine Manifestation.

And the bright angel asks the fetus: "Do you see them?"

And the fetus answers: "I see them."

And the angel then asks: "Do you know who they are?"

And the fetus answers: "I don't know who they are."

And the angel opens his lips and says: "These people whom you see in splendor and glory were created just like you in their mothers' innards and they were born in pain and they lived in the world among mortal men. However, they always did the will of the Almighty, who created them. And that is why they deserved to be crowned.

And every evening, the sad angel takes the fetus and carries it to Gehenna and points to the wicked, who are tortured with eternal sufferings and are drowned in the Abyss of Shame. And their faces are darkened and their eyes are without hope, and their voices are choked with lamenting.

And the angel asks the fetus: "Do you see them?"

And the fetus answers: "I see them."

And the angel then asks: "Do you know who they are?"

And the fetus answers: "I don't know who they are."

And the angel opens his lips and says: "These people whom you see in shame and suffering were created just like you in their mothers' innards and they were born in pain and they lived in the world among mortal men. But they did not do the will of Him who Created them, and so they are condemned to eternal darkness and gnashing of teeth.

"And now know that you too are about to be born and that you will live in the same world. And you will be allowed to choose the path you will take."

Every day, both angels, the bright one and the sad one, carry the newly created fetus around, showing it the world, from one end to the other. And the fetus takes in all voices and noises, all signs and colors, and it sees and hears all the joys and sorrows of the world.

And every night, the two angels light a candle on the fetus's head and teach it the entire Torah and reveal all secrets that have been hidden since the Six Days of Creation, and the two angels lift the edge of the curtain of Eternity, so that the fetus may see.

And when the nine months are over, the angel named Laila comes to the child and asks him: "Do you recognize me?"

And the child answers: "I recognize you." And then the child asks: "Why have you come to me at this time?"

And the angel answers him: "The hour of your birth has come. You have to go into the human world."

And the child says: "I'm very content in the world I'm living in. And if that will be God's will, I beg you: Don't take me to the sinful world of unknowing mortals for I am pure of sin and all-knowing."

And the angel answers him: "The world I'm taking you to

is a world of life and righteousness, and when you were created, the Holy Blessed Be He destined you for that world."

And the child weeps, and his weeping can be heard from one end of the universe to the other. And his weeping is joined by the weeping of all the other embryos in their mothers' innards and also the angels and the seraphim.

But the Almighty does not listen to their weeping.

And the angel named Laila puts out the candle on the baby's head and takes away the two angels, the bright one and the sad one. And then comes Purah, the Angel of Forgetfulness, and he snaps his fingers on the baby's lips, and the baby promptly forgets everything he has seen and heard. And the Torah vanishes from his mind, what he has learned and what he has seen under the edge of the curtain of Eternity. And all that remains of everything he has seen and learned is an echo in the deepest recesses of his heart.

And the angel named Laila forces him out of his mother's innards.

And from that day on, a human being goes through seven worlds.

In the first world, he is like a newly crowned emperor, who is welcomed by all, greeted with joy and with gifts.

In the second world, he is like a billy goat, who feeds on muck, capers about cheerful and carefree, and devours grass that he hasn't sown.

In the third world, he is like a young colt, who knows no hindrances, and is intoxicated with freedom and passion.

In the fourth world, he is like a swift horse, who runs merrily in its harness and doesn't feel the weight of the wagon and the light passengers.

In the fifth world, he is like a donkey, who is burdened with a load and struggles under the driver's lashes.

In the sixth world, he is like a dog, who shamelessly drags everything it can and barks at anyone who comes close.

In the seventh world, he is like a monkey, who looks like a human being and yet is not the same as a human, and it acts crazy, so that everyone laughs at it and no one heeds it.

And then comes the hour of a person's death.

And once again the angel named Laila comes to him and asks him: "Do you recognize me?"

And the person answers: "I recognize you." And the person asks: "Why have you come to me at this hour?"

And the angel answers: "I've come to take you from the world. The hour of your death has arrived."

But the person doesn't want to leave the world and he says: "You took me out of two worlds that I didn't want to leave. Why have you come to take me out of this world?"

And he weeps bitterly and shouts, and his shouting resounds from one end of the world to the other, but not a living soul hears him, for every heart would shatter. And only the night rooster hears the shouting and responds.

And the angel known as Laila tells the person: "Know that you were created by force, you lived by force, and you will die by force, and you will have to account to the King of All Kings, blessed be His Name!"

And the angel takes away the person's soul.

The Creation Melody

(Folktale)

The Chasidim of Tálne sing a cheerful melody, which they call "The Creation Melody." This, they say, is how the melody was composed and how it got its name:

When they were building the great synagogue in Tálne, they suddenly realized that they didn't have enough money to finish the construction.

So the community prepared a large banquet, a tremendous feast, with all sorts of wonderful things—the most exquisite foods, the most extravagant liquors; and all the townsfolk were invited. Now when they were full, merry, and enthusiastic, the town rabbi asked them to pledge donations to complete the synagogue. Each then gave according to his ability—some a lot, some a little.

One of the diners at this religious festivity was the famous musician Yósele, the personal cantor of Rabbi Dúvidl of Tálne. Yósele entertained the company with the full force of his marvelous voice, crooning various Chasidic melodies and Sabbath tunes. He was an enormous success, the guests couldn't get enough of him and kept demanding more and more encores. Eventually Yósele grew so tired that he could no longer perform.

But now, one of the parvenus stood up. He was a bit tipsy, and with the breeziness of the rich he cried out: "If Yósele comes up with a brand-new melody within precisely five minutes, I will contribute another eighteen times eighteen rubles to the completion fund."

Yósele closed his eyes, bowing his head and putting his hands over his ears to drown out the surrounding commotion. He sat there, lost in thought, for several minutes. Then he launched into a brand-new melody, a joyful piece. His singing was ecstatic, rapturous, passionate, and so infectious that everyone started dancing.

The wealthy man kept his promise on the spot, forking over the sum that he had pledged.

Yósele titled his new composition himself: "The Creation Melody." And he sang it so often with the parishioners that they all learned it by heart.

They sang the melody when they inaugurated the new synagogue and also when they brought over the scrolls of the Torah.

The Ten Signs of the Messiah

S. Ansky

(1911)

1

1. God, the Holy Blessed Be He, in His grace, prepared the remedy for the plague.
2. And before He created the world in His holy wisdom, He created the Messiah, the righteous Redeemer.
3. So that in the days of fearful trials and temptations, the Redeemer might save the creatures of the world from the ultimate destruction.
4. But the Almighty concealed any trace of him from human eyes—the day of the Messiah for hundreds and thousands of years.
5. And in the dark hour of God's wrath, when the Temple was destroyed and the nation of Israel was driven from its holy land—
6. The Messiah took two steps out of his concealment, in order to go down to the world and save the survivors of the House of Jacob.

7. But the Almighty, for whom coming events are open until the end of generations, stopped him at his third step and spoke:

8. "The sins of the people of Israel, from today's generation to the future ones, will put your neck in an iron yoke.

9. "And as in an ox in strenuous pain, your eyes will be snuffed and your tongue will cleave to your palate. Will you take that tribulation upon yourself?"

10. And the Messiah asked: "How long will the tribulation last?"

11. And God's voice spoke: "I swear by your life that I have placed the burden on your shoulders for only the length of seven days.

12. "But if your heart grieves, then in my wrath I will wipe out those who hold up your coming!"

13. And the Messiah replied: "God Almighty! With great joy and with all my heart I take the sufferings of the world upon myself.

14. "But not a single life of any of your children should be snuffed."

15. And the Almighty put iron beams on the Messiah's shoulders and a heavy yoke around his neck so that his mighty stature bent down to the ground.

16. And the Messiah began weeping under the heavy weight of his bent stature and he cried out:

17. "God Almighty! How great is my strength! How great is my spirit! How great is my might!"

18. And God's voice spoke: "My beloved child, did you not willingly take upon yourself the sufferings of the world, starting with the Six Days of Creation?

19. "Know that since that hour, since My people lost its land, I have not ascended my royal throne.

20. "And the dew of the pitch-black night hovers constantly over my head."

21. And the instant the Messiah heard those words, he cried out: "My sorrow is stilled. It is enough for the slave to be like the Master!"

2

1. Even morning, with the rising of the morning star, the Almighty shrouds his face in grief and weeps.
2. And His voice, like the voice of a dove, laments and speaks:
3. "Alas! I have destroyed my house, I have burned down my palace and sent my children to wander homeless among alien nations!"
4. And, as he weeps, two tears roll from his eyes and fall into the ocean.
5. And as they fall into the ocean, the tears lament, and their lament is heard from one end of the world to the other.
6. And the heavens shake and the earth quakes.
7. And upon hearing God's cries from the sky, and from the sea the lament of his holy tears, and from the earth the sighs of the embittered people of Israel—
8. The Messiah approaches the lowest step of the Throne of Glory.
9. And he raises his eyes to God and asks with wordless grief: "How much longer, Lord of the Universe?"
10. And the Almighty's eyes grow moist with pity, but His voice answers the Messiah:
11. "My beloved child! Your hour has not yet come, and the time of earthly strength is not yet fulfilled."
12. And every day at noon, the Messiah, in the guise of a pauper, sits among beggars and cripples at the gates of the city of Rome."
13. His clothes are rags and his body is covered with sores.
14. And he unwraps his bandages, exposing his sores one by one to the eyes of the passersby.
15. But none of the nations of the world looks at him and none of their hearts responds to his sores with a shiver of pity.
16. And every day, with the rising of the evening star, the Messiah stands with girded loins at the gates of the Temple, holding a staff and trembling as he waits for God's order: "Go!"
17. And hundreds of years vanish, and thousands of years go by, and the oracular voice remains still.

18. But the time of the Messiah is already nigh, and God's day is already reaching its zenith.

1. And it will happen in the final days:
2. When the hour of the Messiah comes, God will inflict dreadful tribulations on the world,
3. In order to cleanse humanity, just as heavy seeds in a barn are cleansed of chaff,
4. And just as a goldsmith purifies gold of dross in a blazing fire.
5. And the Almighty will inflict terrible signs on the world.
6. And their number will be ten.

1. The first sign will be the sign of great terror.
2. The Almighty will send a hailstorm of stones from the sky and a flood of fire.
3. Rivers and oceans will overflow their shores.
4. Fiery serpents and long-tailed stars will appear in the skies.
5. The foundations of the earth will start to shake, and horrible noises and tumults will be heard.
6. And wild beasts will lose their fear of man.
7. The breasts of the earth will dry up.
8. And a great fear will pounce on human beings.
9. All faces will grow pale, all ankles will stumble in terror, and all hearts will turn as soft as wax.
10. And some people will go about, trembling like drunkards, and they will say:
11. "The final days have arrived. The sufferings of the millennium are drawing nigh!
12. "Woe is us! Who will help us survive the birth pangs of these terrible days?"

5

1. The second sign will be the sign of sun and bloody dew.
2. The Almighty will draw the sun from its sheathe, and a terrible heat will come.
3. And the sinners and false believers will be unable to withstand the heat and they will shout:
4. "Woe is us! Where can we escape the fiery sun?"
5. And they will hide in thornbushes, in ditches, in rocky fissures.
6. But nowhere will they find any cool relief.
7. And they will dig their own graves and lie down in them fully alive and call for death as a redeemer.
8. And after thirty days of heat, the sun will hide its face.
9. And a pitch-blackness will spread across the world.
10. And the sinners and false believers will inhale the darkness.
11. And their bowels will be filled with murk and their bodies will be covered with the foul-smelling mange.
12. And their minds will be muddled and they will be drunk without wine.
13. And those who remain lucid will be ashamed.
14. For they will understand that the signs mean that the redemption is at hand for the people of Israel.
15. And after thirty days of pitch-blackness, the sun will regain its normal illumination.
16. Then the Almighty will send a bloody dew, and bloody ponds and rivers will overflow.
17. The sinners and false believers will forget the difference between blood and water and they will drink from the bloody ponds and rivers.
18. And they will writhe in great pain and curse the day they were conceived.
19. And they will fall in heaps, and there will be no one to bury them.
20. And the cities will be filled with the stench of carcasses.
21. And the buildings and palaces will be devastated, the places of dancing and dining.

6

1. The third sign will be the sign of sealed gates.
2. The Almighty will seal the gates of wisdom, and righteous people will be unable to remain in the world.
3. And they will gather in hosts and go off into the desert.
4. And they will settle among thornbushes and in rocky fissures and in high places and in low valleys, where there are no human settlements.
5. And they will say to the lion: "You are my brother!" And to the leopard: "You are my kinsman!" For they will lose their ties with human beings.
6. And in those days there will be no guide and no ruler for the people of Israel, no loyal shepherds and no truthful men.
7. And false prophets will multiply and seducers of the people.
8. And people will forget the heroes, and the eternal words will be blotted out from all minds.
9. And the synagogues will be emptied and the houses of study will be orphaned, and the houses of worship will be turned into houses of shame.
10. The gates of food will be sealed.
11. And dozens of starvelings will wander around and hold out empty hands, and no heart will respond.
12. For the gates of mercy will also be sealed.

7

1. The fourth sign will be the sign of Gog and Magog.
2. The Almighty will open the gates of the ends of the earth, and from there will come the countless armies of Gog and Magog.
3. They will be vile, wicked, and bloodthirsty.
4. And their appearance will terrify people, and their breath will burn anyone who approaches them.
5. Each of them will have two heads with seven eyes apiece.

6. And they will have the claws of eagles and the teeth of lions and the hind legs of donkeys, and their entire bodies will be covered with hair like those of wild beasts.
7. They will be light and they will run like deer and be bloodthirsty like jackals.
8. Deep oceans will not halt their movement for they will drink up their waters.
9. And dense forests will not halt their running for their teeth will chew up the trees.
10. And children will hide behind their mothers and mothers behind their husbands and husbands behind old men, and they will shout:
11. "Woe is us! Woe is us! Who will save us from the savage armies?"
12. And the old men will reply: "Salvation is at hand, for the day of the Messiah is reaching its zenith."

8

1. The fifth sign will be the sign of three emperors and the Messiah of the House of Joseph.
2. And from the nation of Edom, the Kingdom of Evil, which destroyed the Temple, the Almighty will single out three emperors.
3. These emperors will be false and sinful, but they will pretend to be pious in order to capture human souls.
4. And they will issue evil decrees against the people of Israel and they will force Jews to be false to God.
5. And they will raise the tributes tenfold: the man who has paid five percent will pay fifty, and the man who has paid fifty will pay five hundred, and anyone who cannot pay will be condemned to a brutal death.
6. The three emperors will rule for twenty-seven months in all, each reign will last for nine months.
7. The third emperor will conquer many nations and destroy many countries and he will rule the entire world.

8. And he will inflict even worse persecutions on the people of Israel, and Jews will melt away like wax near fire.
9. And at the end of the reign of the third emperor, the Messiah of the House of Joseph will descend.
10. His name will be Nehemiah son of Hushial, and he will also be named Menahem son of Amiel.
11. And he will bring along the tribes of Ephraim and Menasha and half the tribe of Gad.
12. And the news of the Messiah's coming will be spread, and Jews from all faraway countries will gather around him.
13. And the Messiah of the House of Joseph will go forth against the emperor of Edom, the Kingdom of Evil, and destroy tens of thousands in his army.
14. And he will put the emperor of Edom to the sword and raze his sinful empire to the ground.
15. And he will bring forth from the tower of Emperor Julian the holy implements of the Temple that are concealed there, and he will take them to Jerusalem.
16. And the news of the victories won by the Messiah of the House of Joseph will reach the ears of the emperors of other countries, and they will suffer fear and trembling.
17. And the king of Egypt will conclude eternal peace with the Messiah from the House of Joseph.
18. And the king of Assyria will become his subject and pay tribute.
19. And the Messiah of the House of Joseph will conquer all the countries around Jerusalem, from Damascus to Ashklin.

9

1. The sixth sign will be the sign of Satan Armilus.
2. The Almighty works great wonders.
3. In Rome, the capital of Edom, the Kingdom of Evil, there is the figure of a beautiful woman hewn in marble.
4. And she was not sculpted by human hands, the Almighty created her with His power.

5. And sinners will come from Edom, loathsome and insolent people, and they will lie with the marble woman and they will warm her.

6. And the Almighty will preserve their drops in the woman's marble innards, and a fetus will be created.

7. And when she misses her time, her marble belly will split open, and a creature in human guise will emerge.

8. And his name will be Armilus.

9. And he will be nineteen cubits tall and six cubits broad and his eyes will be a hand's width apart.

10. And he will have two heads, and his hair will be as red as copper.

11. And his eyes will be deep and the soles of his feet will be green.

12. And Armilus will come to Edom, the Kingdom of Evil, and he will say: "I am your god!"

13. And the children of Edom will soon accept him as their god and bow to him and crown him as their king.

14. And Armilus will say to them: "Bring me the Tables of the Law that I gave you."

15. And they will bring the abomination of their idolatry and set it down before him.

16. And he will say: "This is the Torah and these are the Laws that I gave you!"

17. Then Armilus will call for the Messiah of the House of Joseph and the Children of Israel and he will say:

18. "Bring me your Torah and swear to me that I am your god."

19. But the Messiah of the House of Joseph and the Children of Israel will be very angry.

20. And the Messiah of the House of Joseph will unroll a Torah scroll and will read aloud:

21. "I am the Lord, your God, who brought you out of the land of Egypt from the house of bondage.

22. "And ye shall have no other gods but me."

23. And at that same time, the Messiah of the House of Joseph and thirty thousand warriors of the warriors of Ephraim will confront the evil Armilus, and their swords will kill two hundred thousand of his soldiers.

24. And Armilus will fly into a rage, and he will summon the savage armies of Gog and Magog.
25. And he will lead them to the valley ringed by ditches,
26. And he will wage war and he will grow strong and he will put the Jewish army to the sword,
27. And he will imprison the Messiah from the House of Joseph and clap him in irons.
28. And he will torture him with all the dreadful tortures and put him to the sword with an unclean hand.
29. And the Patriarchs will emerge from their rest and welcome the tortured and murdered Messiah from the House of Joseph.
30. And they will pay him the great honor of carrying him on their hands to the Cave of Machpela, where the Patriarchs and Matriarchs lie buried.
31. And they will celebrate his martyrdom for the people of Israel.
32. And the Almighty will welcome him and say:
33. "Ephraim, my loyal son, the child of my love, my compassion for you is great!"
34. And the nations of the world, under the rule of the evil Armilus, will again start persecuting the people of Israel with their evil decrees.
35. And the nations will say: "Have you seen the insolent and hated nation that rose up against the reign of the almighty Armilus and set up their own emperor?"
36. And all the fainthearted and the false believers and the untruthful of the people of Israel will deny the existence of God the Almighty and join the people of Edom, the Kingdom of Evil,
37. And they will jeer at those who will remain steadfast in their faith, and they will say:
38. "Where is the Redemption that you are waiting for, you fools and madmen? The Messiah has fallen under the sword of Armilus the Almighty, so then where will your Redemption come from?"
39. And the survivors of the House of Jacob will suffer fear and affliction, which will make them as pure as gold purified in blazing fire and as holy as the angels.

40. And they will go to the Desert of Judaea and they will stay there for forty-five days, fasting and praying.
41. And Armilus will expand his kingdom and he will wage war against Egypt and conquer it,
42. And he will turn his eyes toward Jerusalem in order to destroy it again for all eternity.

10

1. The seventh sign will be the sign of the first blast of the Shofar (Ram's Horn) of the Messiah.
2. The archangel Michael will come down to earth and will blow the Shofar three times.
3. And at the first blast, all the seven heavens will be filled with joy, and the face of the earth will revive.
4. Seven strokes of interwoven lightning will flash toward David King of Israel,
5. And King David will come from his heavenly palace, and all the later kings of the House of David and the House of Israel will come forth with him.
6. And each king will have a gold crown on his head, but King David's crown will shine brightest of all.
7. And King David will enter the Temple, which will have moved up to heaven, and he will sit on a fiery royal throne.
8. And the kings of the House of David will stand at his right hand and the kings of the House of Israel will stand at his left hand,
9. And he will begin to sing psalms that no living soul has heard.
10. And Metatron, the Angel of Internal Affairs, and all the celestial hosts and the seraphim and the ministering angels and the sacred beasts—they will all reply together:
11. "Holy, holy, holy, Lord of Hosts! Holy, holy, holy, God of Hosts!"
12. And the prophet Elijah will come down to earth and he will stand on the mountains of the Holy Land and he will start to lament about them.

13. And his voice will be heard from one end of the world to the other, and he will say:
14. "Mountains of the Holy Land of Israel, how long will you remain an unfruitful wilderness?"
15. And then he will add: "Peace is coming to the world."
16. And on the second day, he will again climb the mountains and he will say: "Blessing is coming to the world!"
17. And on the third day, he will once again climb the mountains and he will say: "A salvation is coming to the world."
18. And at that same hour, the Almighty will show His vast grace to the Messiah of the House of David; He will remove the yoke from his neck and the iron load from his shoulders.
19. And the Almighty will say: "My beloved child! Your hour has come. Go!"
20. And the Messiah of the House of David will straighten his bent stature and he will take the third step, which was halted for thousands of years,
21. And he will come to the earth in the guise of a pauper riding on a donkey.
22. And the Messiah of the House of David will be accompanied by the prophet Elijah and the prophets Moses, Isaiah, Jeremiah, Baruch, Ezra, Enoch, and the kings of righteousness.
23. All of them will come together with the Messiah of the House of David.
24. And they will bring along the righteous who will have spent forty-five days in the Desert of Judaea, fasting and praying.
25. And the Messiah of the House of David will return their crumbled hearts and will support their weakened arms and will strengthen their stumbling loins.
26. And when the Children of Israel, scattered in strange lands, hear the blast of the Shofar of the Messiah, they will understand that the Redemption has come.
27. And they will gather together and come to the Messiah of the House of David, as it is written:
28. "And there will come those lost in the land of Assyria and those forlorn in the land of Egypt."
29. And the Messiah of the House of David and, with him, the prophet Elijah and the other prophets, will lead the righteous

from the Desert of Judaea, and the Jews who have come from all the corners of the world—will lead them to Jerusalem.

30. And the Messiah of the House of David will mount the last remaining step of the Temple and will sit on it in deep mourning.

31. And the evil Armilus will learn that a king has risen from the people of Israel and he will shout in great fury:

32. "How much longer will the insolent and despised nation rebel against my commandment?"

33. And he will once more gather the armies of Gog and Magog and wage war against the Messiah of the House of David.

34. And both armies will clash in the Valley of Yehoshafat [God the Judge], one from one side and one from the other side.

35. And then God Blessed Be He, in His might and strength, will wage war against the evil Armilus and his hosts,

36. And He will put the Messiah of the House of David at His right hand and the Jewish hosts by his left hand,

37. And He will send a hailstorm of stones and fiery arrows from heaven and a rainfall of boiling pitch and sulfur,

38. And He will destroy Armilus and his hosts down to the very last man,

39. And He will lay waste the evil kingdom of Edom and raze it to the ground, so that no one will know its location until the end of generations.

11

1. The eighth sign will be the sign of the second blast of the Shofar of the Messiah and the Resurrection of the Dead.

2. The archangel Michael will blow the Shofar a second time.

3. And the graves will open up and the stone caverns and the wooden coffins

4. And the martyrs who were tortured and murdered for the Sanctification of the Name will rise from their graves.

5. And all the dead and the stillborn since the Six Days of Creation will come alive.

6. And all the dead will be resurrected in the same form in which they died.
7. The man who was blind in life will be blind, the man who was lame will be lame, the man who was mute will be mute,
8. So that one friend may recognize another and one kinsman another,
9. And so that the wicked may not say that these are newborn and are not resurrected from the dead.
10. And then all defects will be healed and all the sick will be cured.
11. And the Messiah of the House of David, together with the prophet Elijah and all the other prophets will go to the grave of the Messiah of the House of Joseph,
12. And they will bring him back to life, and he will join their ranks with great honor.
13. And the host of prophets will consist of ten.

12

1. The ninth sign will be the sign of the third blast of the Shofar of the Messiah and the redemption from exile.
2. The archangel Michael will blow the Shofar a third time.
3. And from all corners of the world the Children of Israel will gather around the Messiah of the House of David.
4. And from beyond the Gozen River and the faraway cities of Media, the Almighty will lead the ten tribes, who were driven out.
5. And from beyond the Sambatyon River and the Mountains of Darkness, he will lead the children of Moses our Teacher.
6. And the Messiah of the House of David will go to the Holy Land, leading all the living Jews and all the resurrected,
7. Those who are far and those who are near, the righteous and the penitent, down to the very last one.
8. And the Almighty will set up seven canopies of precious stones over the Messiah of the House of David,

9. And from under every canopy four rivers will flow out: a river of milk, of honey, of wine, and of finest spices.
10. And the Almighty will take the ewer of oil from the hands of the prophet Elijah,
11. And He will anoint the Messiah of the House of David as king and lead him under the canopies.
12. And the Almighty will emerge before everyone in his great glory,
13. And he will be followed by the Messiah of the House of David and King David together with the other angels and behind them the prophets.
14. And the Torah will be at the Messiah's right hand, and the entire people of Israel at his left hand,
15. And each tribe will be surrounded by a luminous cloud.
16. And in front of them a land will spread out, blossoming like God's Garden of Eden.

13

1. The tenth sign will be the sign of Jerusalem the Exalted and of God's dominion over the world.
2. The Almighty will gather together all the mountains in the world and pile them atop one another.
3. And on the uppermost peak He will place the new Jerusalem, Jerusalem the Supreme.
4. And He will surround it with lofty walls of earth, with gates and towers of wondrous beauty.
5. And the new Jerusalem will be set up on ten stones.
6. And these are their names: ruby, topaz, agate, emerald, onyx, jasper, sapphire, opal, tourmaline, beryl.
7. And the Almighty will add two stones, carbuncle and turquoise, so that there will be twelve, one for each tribe.
8. And the Almighty will put up the Temple in all its brilliance and splendor.
9. And in its glory it will surpass the First Temple, the Temple of King Solomon.

10. And the heavens and the earth and the people of Israel will be as new.
11. The heavens and the earth, which will be closed like a book or folded like a garment in the fearful days of the Messiah, will be straightened out.
12. And the people of Israel, going through baseness and death, will be reborn and revived.
13. And the Almighty will increase the light of the sun seven times seven times sevenfold and altogether three hundred forty-three times.
14. And the light of the moon will be increased to the same degree.
15. But the light of the righteous will be six hundred forty-three times brighter than the light of the sun at its zenith.
16. And the whole wondrous beauty of the earth, which withered after Adam's sin, will be revived.
17. And every day the earth will sprout new plants and yield new fruits.
18. And the Almighty in his vast grace will feel pity for Sodom and Gomorrah and will resurrect them from their ruins and restore them in their former splendor.
19. And the Almighty will cast Satan the Annihilator and the hosts of his accusers and destroyers into the eternal flames of the depths of the underworld, and they will be doomed there forever.
20. And the Almighty will slaughter the Angel of Death, and the human race will become immortal.

14

1. God, the Holy Blessed Be He, will put a new spirit in the old words and will give the human race a new Torah.
2. And He will send all the nations in the world the understanding of Truth and Righteousness.
3. And He will open for all the nations in the world the wellspring of Truth and Goodness,

4. In order to bring about what has been said:
5. "And I will give you new hearts and put a new spirit in you.
6. "And I will remove the hearts of stone from your bodies and I will give you hearts of flesh and blood."

The Shepherd's Melody

(Folktale)

❧

In 1769, during the days of Gonte's slaughters of Jews, a tsáddik (Chasidic rabbi) named Leyb lived in the very tiny shtetl of Pilyáve in Podólye.

The local Jews still know a lot of stories about him, and they talk about his strict piety, his great humility, and his profound righteousness. They even believe that it was because of him that Pilyáve was spared the horrors inflicted by Gonte and his murderous troops.

Rabbi Leyb was devoted to his people, loving and befriending each and every one of them. And the Jews circulated an utterance of his that he often repeated: "An incomplete tsáddik loves incomplete rogues, a complete tsáddik also loves complete rogues."

The rabbi had many followers and many disciples. His task was to visit the various Jewish communities and persuade the parents to send their children to study the Torah.

Now legend has it that when he and some of his students were rolling along a country road, they saw a Christian boy, a shepherd, who was blowing his pipe. When they drew near, and Rabbi Leyb heard the music, he told the driver to stop the wagon. The rabbi then listened closely to the tune emerging from the shepherd's pipe.

When the boy stopped, the rabbi gave him some coins so that he might repeat his song. And the rabbi had him play it several times until he and his disciples had learned the melody and could sing it for themselves. But once they were able to sing the entire melody correctly, the shepherd got all mixed up, and in the end he began playing an entirely different melody.

Gehenna

S. Ansky

(1908)

1

High above the seven heavens,
High above the earth and stars,
Everything that God the Ruler,
The Almighty and All-Powerful,
Once created with compassion
And with grace or with the fiery
Utterance of wrath—one judgment
Reigns alone, a cold, strict Law,
Never changing, everlasting.
It is written: "Measure for measure:
An eye for an eye, a tooth for a tooth!"
A God-fearing pious life
Is rewarded with the Hereafter,
In the radiant Garden of Eden.
But for erring and for sinning
You will suffer all the sufferings
Of the Seven Halls of Hell.

Deep is Hell and dark is Hell,
No repentance here will help,
Not a tear or prayer from here
Reaches God the Ruler's feet.
Here you feel that death is mercy,
Silent non-existence—but
For the sinners in Gehenna
Death has no dominion here.
Amid vile and venomous laughter
Sammael and all his minions
Yell and sigh and moan and scream
Evermore and never less.

Three roads lead to the Gates of Hell.
One road runs through the abysses
Of the seven seas on earth.
And the second road runs like
Signs of shame, a hangman's lashes,
Through the desert, dead and waste.
And the third road, the most dire,
Long and dark and dreadful, runs
Underground to the Gates of Hell.
Anywhere a Jew may die,
Once he suffers his demise
And the punishments in his grave
He will roll beneath the ground,
With no road through deepest gloom,
Tearing through the hardest rocks,
Through the walls and through the swamps
Till he finds the Holy Land.
And from there the road then runs
Underneath the raging river,
The Sambatyon, yes, and then
Under all the Mountains of Darkness.

At the gates of Hell, Gehenna,
Lurk the countless hosts of demons,
Welcoming the sinner with
Wild and raucous noise and laughter.

First of all, at his arrival,
Every sinner must confess
All the sins that he committed,
All the wrongs that he once did,
Did to God and did to others.
He himself must tell his story:
Where and when he did his misdeeds.
And whenever he recalls
Any sin or any wrong,
A new demon is created,
And he tortures and torments
The sinner for creating him.

When a month of hellish anguish,
Hellish agony is over,
Then the sinner's body is
Chomped and chewed up by the teeth
Of the worst of the destroyers,
Ground into the finest dust.
And the dust is scattered on
All the roads in Paradise,
Where the righteous tread upon it.
Then the sinner's body is
Recreated. And a bitter
Wailing cuts through all the yelling:
"God in heaven, God is true,
"True His judgment, true His sentence.
"For our sins we all deserve
"All these tortures, all these torments.
"Praised be God the Ruler—while we
"Suffer everlasting shame."

2

Six full days and nights, till Sabbath,
Hell keeps burning, Hell keeps boiling

With the wrath of the Creator,
Hell is shut to all forgiveness,
Hell is closed to all compassion.
But the moment Sabbath starts,
Hell calms down, and all the devils
And destroyers promptly vanish.
All the flames and all the fires
In the lime kilns are snuffed out.
And an angel mild, a messenger,
Flies from Heaven down to Hell,
Bringing comfort, solace, pity.
With his wing he fans burnt bodies
And he eases all their sufferings
And he salves their injuries,
Using Eden's oil and spices.
Mercifully the angel whispers,
Fanning faith in God's forgiveness.
And from Heaven, consolation
And the spirit of Holy Sabbath
Now descend upon the sinners.
But the moment stars appear,
Holy Sabbath is ushered out,
And the flames must blaze afresh
And the tortures start anew,
All the torments of Gehenna.

Still the angel sent from Eden
Does not carry Sabbath peace
Or the spices and the solace
For all sinners in Gehenna.
Anyone who ever dared
To blaspheme against God's name—
He receives no peace of mind
Even though it's Holy Sabbath,
The mild angel sent from Eden
Brings no balm and gives no comfort
To the sinner in his sufferings.

This is the description now
Of Gehenna's Seven Hells:

3

The first Hell is Bor (the Pit).
There amid an icy cold
An infernal fire burns,
And tremendous rivers flow,
Filled with seething pitch and sulfur.
Glowing coals are strewn about,
Huge as fiery rocks and mountains.
Devils, demons, and destroyers
Have the insolent faces of
Scorpions and snakes and serpents,
And no magic spells protect you
When these monsters pounce upon you.
And this Hell reverberates
With loud ranting, raving, railing.
Burning bodies writhe alive
In their tortures, in their torments,
Boiling in the fires and kettles.
There a demon drives a sinner
With his fiery whips and lashes
Up a coal, a blazing mountain.
And he clambers breathlessly
Till he climbs upon the peak,
And from there he swiftly dives
Into a sea of pitch and sulfur.
Other sinners writhe and wriggle,
Eaten up alive by worms.
Others still are hung aloft
By their fingers, by their innards,
By their tongues, their hearts, their eyes.
And the scorpions and the serpents
Twist and turn and twirl and dart,

Bringing a disgusting stench,
Bringing venom on their breath.

In the first Hell you will find
Sinners who did not perform
All the Holy Rites correctly:
Those who studied Torah with no
Ecstasy and no elation,
Those who never showed respect by
Standing for the elderly,
Those who were not kind and cordial
When they gave an alms or present
To a pauper in distress.
Women too are tortured here,
Those who were not chaste enough
To piously cover their hair,
Those who did not teach their children
To confess, pray, shout: "Amen,
"May His Name be magnified!"

4

In the second Hell, called Shakhat
(Pitfall), stand the endless rows of
Snowy mountains, fiery mountains,
And the hornèd demons hurl
Sinners from snow into fire
And from fire into snow.
And in each and every second
The sinner's flesh is burned and frozen.
And he constantly keeps craving
Light and warmth or cold and darkness.

Here you'll find the Jews who doubted,
Wavered between good and evil,
Frivolously changed a promise,

Tittle-tattled during prayers.
Also Jews who hurt a friend
With a snide remark, with malice,
Deeply shaming him so that
His face turned every living color.

5

The third Hell is Dumah (Grave).
In an icy, lifeless silence,
In a gray, unstirring stillness,
Which was made before the birth of
Any sound in God's creation,
Dreadful terror lies in wait,
Lurking like a beast of prey.
And he peers, devoid of eyes,
Gaping blindly at all things
With a look of utter madness.

In the midst of deathly hush,
Strongest fires fade and flicker,
Wane and weaken, gutter, wither.
Hard rocks, boulders, iron cliffs
Lose their strength and sturdiness,
Crumbling into shards and gravel,
Feebly scattering abroad.
Deeply filled with dread and terror
Of unstirring hush and silence,
Every sinner starts to break
Every bone in his own body
Just to interrupt the deathly
Stillness with a sound, a noise.
But no use—inside this Hell
Every sound is dead or stillborn.

Here, this icy hush contains
All the proud and arrogant Jews,
Those who cloaked their empty souls in
Haughty, sanctimonious silence,
Those who felt no pity when they
Saw that other Jews were suffering.
People who forgot the "not" in
God's commandment: "Do not hold the
"Worker's wages overnight."
Those who shamelessly gorged and guzzled
And made merry and caroused
In a place where there were paupers.

6

The fourth of the Seven Hells is
Tit Ha-Yoveyn (Place of Suffering).
In an endless hush the sinner's
Slowly plunged into a swamp of
Heavy filth and stench and sickness . . .
He keeps struggling to find
Something to hold on to there
For a minute or forever,
But he never ever finds it.
He keeps seeing rocks and branches,
Powerful restraints before him.
But when he then reaches out,
They all vanish from his sight.
Demon hands, a hundred thousand,
Swiftly hold out heavy sticks—
But just as he tries to grab them,
All the sticks then crack and crumble
Like dry branches. And he sinks,
Sinks into the deep abyss,
Nothing to hold on to there
For a minute or forever.

Those who sink here are the ones who
Bore false witness, perjurers;
Those who never lent a hand
To the poor, the weak, the weary;
Those who, vicious, insolent,
Leaped down from the lofty heights
Of the fortress of the Torah
To the deep and dull abyss of
Inquiry and sophistry;
Those who with glib flattery,
With a glance, a word, a gesture,
Coaxed a decent girl or wife
Into doing evil deeds.

7

The fifth Hell is Sheól (Abyss).
There five kinds of fires burn.
The first fire is a liquid:
Fiery rivers rush and roar and
Rage into the fiery seas.
And the second fire blazes
In the fiery hurricanes.
The third fire flares and flames
In the huge and mighty deserts
Filled with fiery sand like sparks,
Sand that rises and that flies
In the dense and fiery clouds.
The fourth fire drops like snowflakes,
Covering mountains, filling valleys
With its burning-icy flames.
The fifth is a silent fire,
Blue and frozen in its stillness.
This is the most horrible fire.
It consumes, devours fire
In the fiery abyss,

Pouring flames upon the sinner,
Flames like gushing blood upon him,
Flowing into all his limbs,
Storming through with all inflictions,
With infernal agonies.
And the sinner burns and blazes
In dark lust and in wild passion
That are never quenched in him.

This is where the sinners suffer
Who gave in to flesh and fancy,
To gross coveting and craving:
Never fasted on Yom Kippur
And ate bread at Passover.
And tormented are the others:
Loan sharks who bled paupers white;
Those who gathered massive fortunes
From the sweat and work of others;
Those who on their own or through
Someone else shed innocent blood;
Those who never circumcised
Their sons, never making them
Members of a Jewish parish;
Women who ignored the law
Governing their period.

8

The sixth Hell is called Tsalmovet
(Shadow of Death, Great Darkness):
Boundless murk and emptiness,
No beginning and no bottom.
Dreadful, lifeless nothingness
Was created long before
The Six Days of God's Creation.
In this spaceless hell the sinner

Constantly sees nothing but
His unchanging self before him.
He is driven by a yearning,
By a fierce and frenzied striving
To attain that self of his.
But he cannot reach himself,
And he does not know or grasp:
Who is he? His self or that self?
Or are both of them mere figments
Conjured up by yet another?

In this sixth Hell sinners suffer
Who, though lucid, killed themselves;
Those who with their mockery,
Or their doubts, or their despair,
Drained another person's heart,
Killed his faith in the Creator,
His belief in Truth and Justice;
Those who were informers, traitors;
Those who lied as witnesses,
Murdering an innocent person
Sullying an innocent name
With a lie and with a libel;
Those who were adulterers,
Thus erasing from their faces
God's own image and His likeness;
And tormented are the judges
Who in fear or who for bribes
Handed down dishonest judgments,
And in black mendacity
Covered up the wicked deeds
Of the rich and powerful.

9

And the seventh and the last
Of Gehenna's Seven Hells

Has no name . . . It's been forgotten . . .
A Gehenna in Gehenna,
And a mute and deathly darkness
That was left so long ago
From the Six Days of Creation,
A dense chasm of thick darkness,
Sleeping soundly a deep sleep,
Frozen, rigid like a rock.
And the dreadful Lord's revenge,
His most terrifying wrath,
Burn and blaze and flare and flame
In a black and hellish fire.

There they boil and seethe in kettles,
In a simmering stench—the sinners
Who blasphemed against God's Name,
Desecrated His pure Name,
Strong and sacred and almighty.
For the atheists in this Hell,
Never does the faintest spark of
Pity stir in the Creator.
Never will they have a Sabbath,
Never any jubilee,
Never any fallow year.
And their punishment in Hell
Will not stop in all eternity.
Even if the cosmos shatters,
God will not remember them:
The deniers of the Lord.
And a pitch-black fire hovers
On the gates of this last Hell,
Here the flames are full of dead words:
"God-forsaken, God-forlorn,
"God-forgotten here forever
"In the deepest chasm of darkness."

The Gallows Melody

(Folktale)

Byélo-tsérkov literally means "white church"; but the Jews in the town of that name referred to it as "black abomination."

Now one day, the local cantor and the choir members were slandered by some Christians, who claimed that during the Sabbath ceremony at the great synagogue, the Jews had supposedly cursed the tsar instead of blessing him. So the accused were imprisoned and condemned to death by hanging.

The sentence was to be carried out on a Sunday. Several gallows were put up, and a lot of peasants from the surrounding countryside came with their wives and children to watch the execution of the Jews—the "anti-Christs."

The story goes that as they were being led to the gallows, the victims, in their great sadness and heartbreak, were crooning a passage from the daily Eighteen Benedictions: "And the slanderers shall have no hope." The cantor's voice soared over the heads of the onlookers and across the marketplace, and his chant was supported by the anguished voices of the choir. And they kept singing until they reached the gallows: "And the slanderers shall have no hope."

But now a miracle occurred. The melody touched the hearts of the peasants, both men and women, and weeping could be heard from all sides. The music softened even the stone hearts of the judges, who then rescinded their judgment and released the cantor and the choristers.

The Jews of Byélo-tsérkov memorized that passage about slanderers and sang it on every occasion, whether sad or joyful.

God on Trial

S. Ansky

(1908)

All this happened recently,
In the time when all the world
Resonated with the wonders
Of our Rabbi Elimelekh.

On a dreadful day for Jews,
The emperor of Romania
Suddenly issued a decree:
Every single Jew must leave
His domain within a month.
All the Jews were shocked and shaken
By the emperor's ghastly edict.
And they wept and shrieked and mourned,
And they fasted and they prayed,
And they left no stone unturned.
But these labors were in vain.
Evil spirits, odious demons,
Those who lie in wait for Jews,
Let no tear and let no prayer
Enter heaven, reach the Maker.

One sole Jew in all Romania
Did not fast and did not shriek.
This old man, whose name was Feyvel,
Was renowned among the Jews:
He spent every waking moment
With the Bible and the Talmud
At the house of prayer and study.
Now when Feyvel heard about the
Monarch's villainous decree,
He was terror-stricken too
And he felt like weeping, wailing . . .
But then all at once his mind
Brightened up with an idea.
So he grabbed a Pentateuch,
Hastily consulted it,
And then instantly exclaimed:
"An imperial decree?
"How can that be possible?
"Our Torah says quite clearly:
"Such an edict has no substance!"

And he promptly raced away
(Although it was late at night)
To the rabbi. In those days
All the Jews here in Romania
Were ruled by the great and famous
Tsáddik, Rabbi Elimelekh.
Feyvel woke him from his slumber
And he fiercely yelled at him:

"Rabbi, call a court to order!
"Plain as day our Torah says
"Jews have but a single ruler:
"The Creator of the World.
"So how can an emperor
"Issue fiats against Jews?
"And above all, Rebbe, tell me,

"How can God permit this thing,
"This outrageous infamy?"

"Feyvel, what is it you want?"
Rabbi Elimelekh asked him.

"What I want? I want a trial!
"In regard to this decree
"I would like to try the Maker
"In a Jewish court of law!"

"Listen carefully, my son!"
Elimelekh calmly answered.
"I must tell you, loud and clear,
"That I think it's insolent
"To indict God the Creator,
"For He is a vengeful Judge.
"And you may be courting danger
"If you take the Lord to court . . .
"Still, I fully understand,
"You are risking life and limb
"For a large community.
"So I'm willing to convene
"Our Jewish court of law.
"Midnight is the wrong time, though.
"Come back after morning prayers."

Suddenly that night three guests,
Each a rabbi and a tsáddik
Came to Elimelekh's home.
One guest was the Rabbi of Apt,
Yes, the famous wonder-worker.
Elimelekh then proposed
That they join him as the judges
In tomorrow's litigation.
And the visitors agreed,
Giving him their sacred word.

Early the next morning, when
Feyvel reached the Jewish court,
All four rabbis donned their prayer shawls,
And the court was called to order.
"Feyvel!" cried the Rabbi of Apt.
"We four rabbis do decree
"That you state your grievance now,
"Your complaint against the Maker."
Feyvel, though, was pale, confused,
Stammering and trembling.
"No, you rabbis, no, I can't . . .
"I've lost all my courage now . . .
"I don't feel the inspiration
"That I felt just yesterday . . ."

The presiding judge replied
In a stern, imperious voice:
"I will give you strength and power,
"Insight, yes, and inspiration!
"Have faith! There will be no bias
"In this court and in this trial!"

All at once, the plaintiff felt
A great surge of inspiration,
And he started his indictment.
First he quoted from the Bible,
Then he cited evidence
From the pages of the Talmud,
From rabbinical authority,
Demonstrating clear as day
That the Maker had no right
To allow the evil edict.

Now one of the judges had
An idea, and so he asked
In a mild and quiet tone:
"Feyvel, tell us, why don't you
"Sue the monarch, not the Maker?"

"Monarch! Shmonarch! Ugh! Who cares?"
Feyvel angrily cried out.
"That's a terrible idea!
"Why should I have any dealings
"With the emperor of Romania?
"What is he? A nobody!
"I will only litigate
"With the Maker—God Himself!"

Next the Rabbi of Apt stood up
Proudly and he softly spoke:
"Let the Maker of the World
"Give us now a clear response to
"Feyvel's clear indictment here."

Elimelekh then joined in:
"I will give you the response.
"There is certainly no doubt that
"Feyvel's right in every way:
"All of us, the Children of Israel,
"Are the servants of the Maker.
"He alone, and no one else,
"Has the right to punish us. But
"Like a master with a slave
"God, the Maker, has the right to
"Let a proxy do the punishing!—"
"No, he has no right to do so!"
Feyvel heatedly broke in.
"Are the Jews mere slaves to God?
"Don't forget that it is clearly
"Written: '*Ki bonim Atem*'—
"'For we are Thy children, God!'
"Any father punishes
"All his children personally.
"Not through anybody else!"

"Well, then," Elimelekh asked.
"Tell me: How could Titus burn
"Down the Temple in Jerusalem?"

"A good question! Well, the Temple
"Was a dwelling for the Maker.
"Yes, He did have it destroyed.
"But we know that now the Maker
"Does regret what He once did,
"And the Lord laments so loudly:
"'Woe is me! For I destroyed
"'My own palace with My own hand,
"'Leaving it in ruins and rubble.'"

"Let it be," cried Elimelekh.
"I'll concede your point about
"The Destruction of the Temple.
"But just think about the Jews—
"They are sinners one and all!
"Think how often God the Maker—
"Sometimes mild and sometimes wild—
"Told the Jews to leave their evil
"And to think about repentance!
"Did it help in any way?
"In the end, He lost His temper
"And the Maker hit the roof . . ."

"'Lost his temper? Hit the roof?'"
Feyvel yelled at Elimelekh.
"Just what are you saying there?!
"If we go along with that,
"Then the furious Maker can
"Wipe out all the universe,
"Slaughter every living soul!"

"Don't you see? Of course, He can!"
Elimelekh snapped at Feyvel.

"No, He cannot! No, He must not!"
Feyvel angrily retorted.
"How can that be? If it's so,
"There's no justice and no judge!
"Tell me! Don't we have our Torah?! . . .
"Listen, I must warn you now:
"I won't leave until you issue
"A decree that our Maker,
"Just like any human being,
"Must obey the Torah's laws . . ."

But the Rabbi of Apt then
Put an end to this debate.
He stood up and stroked his beard,
Then he said imperiously:
"Everything is clear to me!
"We can stop our arguing!"
Next the rabbi quickly added:
"There's a custom in our trials:
"When both sides have had their say,
"They must leave our court of law!
"If either party then refuses,
"If he does not leave as ordered,
"He must pay a fine, and then
"He is shamefully removed! . . .
"You too, Lord of all the Worlds,
"Must now leave our court of law! . . ."

Rabbi Elimelekh jumped up:
"What? The Torah clearly says:
" 'Kvode moleh oylem '
"How, I ask, can God depart
"From this place for even an instant?"

For a while the judge kept silent.
Then he raised his thick, gray eyebrows
And he angrily grumbled too.
"Since the Torah clearly states:

"'God is everywhere at once.'
"Please remain with us, oh Lord!
"But we say to You quite clearly:
"In our holy Court of Law,
"Our verdict is impartial.
"Don't forget, please, that the Torah
"Is no longer in the Heavens.
"You once brought it down for us! . . ."

For three days and nights, the judges
Argued, wrangled, and disputed—
Thunderous were their fierce debates!
Inferences from minor to major,
Talmudic laws, analogies,
Cabalistic allegories,
And allusions in the Zohar,
And the mysteries of the Torah
And the numbered words and sayings
Of the holy Baal-Shem-Tov.

For three days and nights, they quibbled
And they squabbled . . . And the rabbis
Yelled and fought and screamed and hollered,
Cursed and swore and vilified,
Called each other vicious names,
"Creep!" and "Jerk!" and "Rat!" and "Blockhead!"
Hurled anathemas at each other!

In the end they compromised:
God, they said, made a mistake,
When he let the emperor issue
His outrageous edict, which
They denounced as null and void:
He must cancel his decree.

Now a scribe wrote down the judgment
Word for word upon a parchment.
All the holy rabbis then

Signed and sealed the document.
And this text was stored among
All the Torah scrolls preserved
In the Ark of the Covenant . . .

Just one day and just one night
Wore away. And then the emperor
Canceled his decree! Amen!

Keeping Watch

S. Ansky

(1916)

Repentance, prayer, and charity
Will avert the evil decree.
(From the Prayer Book)

The Judgment

Between Rosh-ha-Shonah (New Year's Day) and Yom Kippur (the Day of Atonement) come the Days of Awe—the holy and dreadful Ten Days of Repentance. During these ten days, God Blessed Be He opens the great book of all the deeds in the world, every single deed that has been done by every individual and every nation. Everything is appraised and assessed, is weighed and measured. The Holy Blessed Be He judges the world and all its creatures. And the Book of Life records and registers everything that lies in store for each person.

And in the hour of the dreadful judgment, by the lowest step of the Throne of Glory, the holy angels wage a terrible war with the forces of impurity. They are struggling for the fate of the "Single Nation," and God help the people of Israel if the dark forces are victorious! For if these forces win, then Jews can expect all kinds of ordeals and persecutions, libels and massacres. However, even after the judgment is rendered, the Almighty in His vast grace gives the sinful person the possibility of alleviating or even canceling the verdict: the sinner can do so through Prayer, Repentance, and Charity.

But before these three forces can appear before the Throne of Glory, they have to pass through the vestibule of the palace, where their purity and holiness are determined. And if, God forbid, even the slightest flaw is found in them, then Satan and his followers will come and close the Gates of Heaven and not allow the petitioners to reach the Throne of Glory.

The most important of the three is Repentance, next comes Prayer, and finally Charity. But when they reach the vestibule of the palace, they enter in a different sequence. First comes Charity, because its time ends when Yom Kippur begins. After Charity comes Repentance, and then last of all, at sunset, comes Prayer, whereby Ne'ilah is recited to conclude the Day of Atonement.

One year, the war over the fate of the people of Israel was fierce and harsh. It was the time of that giant among giants, the Holy Baal-Shem-Tov, the Master of the Sacred Name, who ruled over angels and seraphim and who exercised a rigorous authority in the Higher Worlds. Satan the Accuser, trembling before the Baal-Shem's power, girded his loins and braced his dark strength. Then, seizing the moment of God's wrath, when the Gates of Compassion were shut, Satan came forth with the full might of the Sitra Akhara—the "Other Side," the Devil's Camp. Now he brought his merciless charges against the people of Israel—and he won! God issued an unusually horrible judgment. And the heavenly forces, shuddering because of what had happened, did not dare object to the verdict. In their great terror, they concealed these events from the radiant eyes of the Holy Baal-Shem-Tov.

In Medzhibuzh, Jews started preparing for Yom Kippur at the crack of dawn. They were already imbued with the grand and dreadful glory of the sacred day. Putting all worldly cares behind them, they shook off the final traces of workaday life. At twelve noon, the farmers' wagons all vanished from the marketplace. The shops hastily closed one by one. Then, the houses. And the more that workaday life disappeared, the more the holy shul (the synagogue) livened up. Their minds clear of everyday thoughts and worries, Jews poured into the shul—dozens of torrents, from all directions. Some of the men wore white linen robes and held wax candles in their hands. Many of the Jews were storekeepers, who, together with their wives and children, had come from the surrounding villages to celebrate the Days of Awe. Strong and healthy, with faces and clothing resembling those of the Christian peasants, these men walked quietly and humbly.

The impoverished shul, covered with a low thatched roof, opened its doors wide to the approaching worshipers. Paupers and cripples were lined up in the courtyard, holding out their hands, while solid burghers with plates and boxes were collecting for all sorts of community needs. And the worshipers, each according to his ability, gave out alms and put coins in the boxes or on the plates. Every Jew donated with a loving smile and with all his heart. Their coins flowed into the beggars' hands, jingled in the boxes, and clattered on the plates.

Little by little, the courtyard emptied out. The paupers, the cripples, and the charity collectors were gone. The very last gift, a penny, had been slipped into a box by a blind beggar woman.

And all Jewish life passed into the shul, which was filled with lustrous ecstasy. Hundreds of men in white robes were thronging together in silent prayer; hundreds of long, straight candles were crowded together, their yellow, flickering flames darting upward. And everything and everyone was spellbound, waiting for the first tiding of the holy Yom Kippur, waiting for Kol Nidre, the evening service initiating this sacred day: "All vows, bonds, promises, obligations, and oaths . . . are absolved . . ."

That morning, the Holy Baal-Shem-Tov had still been at peace. In high spirits and with a luminous face, he blessed his disciples, the crowd, and the children brought to him by their parents. But the closer they got to evening, the more apprehensive he grew. At the final meal before the fast, he sat amid his followers, motionless, profoundly silent, lowering his head, barely touching his food. Only once did he raise his head; his penetrating gaze rested on Dovid Pirkes, who was supposed to lead the Kol Nidre prayer at the lectern. Under the holy rebbe's piercing eyes, Dovid Pirkes began shivering and again and again he examined the most secret nooks and crannies of his heart, intent on finding a flaw. But he found none.

Whereupon the Holy Baal-Shem left for synagogue. Once outdoors he happened to look up at the sky and saw that it was overcast with thick, black clouds like steel armor. He was terror-stricken. And when he entered the shul and stood at the lectern, his face was covered with a cloud that was darker and denser than the clouds in the heavens.

His disciples, in fear and trembling, scrutinized the rebbe's every last gesture, and their hearts grew heavier and heavier. However, their faith was bolstered by their confidence in the great strength of the Holy Baal-Shem, and so they waited and hoped . . .

Dovid Pirkes, cut off from the world, separated from all material things, quite prepared to sacrifice himself for his people, stood by the lectern, waiting for the Baal-Shem to signal the start of Kol Nidre.

But the Holy Baal-Shem stood there as if turned to stone. His face, utterly blank, was chalky white and bathed in cold sweat. And two streams of tears were running down his cheeks.

He kept silent, as if forgetting where he was and what this hour was. And everyone around him waited, breathless and alarmed. Minutes crept by like hours, and hours crawled past like years. But still the Baal-Shem made no sign. Now the anxiety turned into fear, and the fear turned into terror, and hundreds of hearts were filled with a pain that was about to erupt in a clamorous lament.

Charity

From all directions, snow-white angels, mild and still, came flying into the vestibule of the palace, bearing Jewish alms, small coins, food and clothes. Everything they brought was as shiny as fine gold, as glittery as diamonds. And joyously they arrived at the Throne of Glory. The angels cautiously gathered every crumb of bread, every tiny thread of tattered garments, every coin no matter how tiny. But the mound was small and poor because the nation of Israel was destitute and dejected.

When the last angel had flown in with the last alms (the blind beggar woman's penny), who should appear at the threshold of the palace vestibule but Satan the Accuser. Smugly exulting in his victory, he shredded the curtain with his black wings, to expose a tableau, in which each second brought a new day, a new week, a new month, a new year.

There was a Jewish storekeeper, a man burdened with many children. His business was getting worse and worse, and when the annual interest installment fell due on his loan from the Christian landowner, he had no money to pay it. He begged for an extension until the next deadline, promising to pay the interest for both years at that time. But the next year, he again had no money. Now his creditor grew angry and, following the custom of that period, he put the storekeeper's entire family in the dungeon. He allowed only the debtor himself to remain free so that he might lay hold of enough money to get his wife and children out. The landowner then told the Jew that if he didn't receive the cash within three months, he would stop lowering the bread and water to the mother and children and let them starve to death.

The storekeeper became a beggar, asking for alms, wandering from town to town, village to village, telling everyone about his great misfortune. Jews, the "merciful sons of merciful fathers," gave him alms, but they couldn't donate the full sum because his debt was huge and the Jews were poor. The storekeeper wandered for one week, for two, for one month, for two, roaming further and further from his home. His body grew tired, and his legs started to buckle. He managed to save up a few rubles, but that was only a tiny fraction of what he needed; and so the storekeeper was overcome with great despair. One day, when he was wandering, hungry and weary, he suddenly heard some noises—a cracking of whips a pounding of hooves. Before he could turn his head, a bunch of cossacks came galloping tempestuously, leading a coach drawn by eight horses in tandem. With a lash of his whip, one of the cossacks flung the beggar into a ditch, and the riders dashed on. However, Prince Saguszko, who was sitting inside the coach, had his driver stop, and he ordered his men to pick up the Jew and bring him over.

When the bloody storekeeper was brought to the coach, the prince asked him where he was from and where he was going. The storekeeper told him about his great misfortune.

After hearing him out, the prince asked: "How long have you been wandering and begging?"

"For two months now."

"How much have you collected?"

"Ten rubles."

"And how much do you have to pay your debtor?"

"Three hundred."

The prince burst out laughing. Then he told a servant to put three hundred gold rubles into a pouch, tossed it over to the storekeeper, and quickly took off again.

The instant the prince tossed over the bag of gold, Satan the Accuser grabbed it and hurled it over to the mound of Jewish alms. The rubles shone with a golden glow and jingled with a golden sound throughout the palace vestibule, and their glistening snuffed out the tiny Jewish coins, making them small and poor, and Satan was about to kick the Jewish alms out of the palace vestibule.

At that very instant, the Baal-Shem, as if awakening, turned toward the panicky men who were standing there in their white robes. And the Baal-Shem asked them: "Where is the storekeeper from Maloyarov? Bring him here!"

The worshipers, shaken by these unexpected words, all assumed that the storekeeper must have committed a horrible sin, which prevented them from starting Kol Nidre. And so hundreds of eyes glared at him.

A strong, healthy Jew with a rustic face left the wall where he was standing. He glanced around in naive fear, took several steps, then paused in helpless amazement.

"Come here, don't be afraid!" the Baal-Shem ordered him with a warm look.

Trudging in his big peasant boots, the storekeeper headed unsteadily toward the Baal-Shem.

"Tell me, Chaim," the Baal-Shem turned to him, "you knew Prince Saguszko's reddish dog, didn't you?"

"The prince's reddish dog?" The storekeeper was so confused by this unforeseen question that he couldn't answer. It was only when the Baal-Shem repeated his words that the storekeeper managed to reply: "The prince's reddish dog? Who didn't know him? Everybody knew him."

"Then tell us what happened to him."

"Well, he was an excellent dog," the storekeeper began. "The prince bought him for a thousand rubles and never went anywhere without him. But once, when the prince had very important guests, the dog barked at them and jumped on them, and so the prince grabbed a rifle and he shot and killed the dog."

"Killed?" The Baal-Shem was astounded. "How could such a cherished dog annoy him? He paid a thousand rubles for him?"

"A thousand rubles?! That's nothing for the prince!" the storekeeper replied.

The Holy Baal-Shem straightened up, turned to the others, and said: "Do you hear, you Jews? For Prince Saguszko a thousand rubles is nothing—much less three hundred rubles. That's a pittance for him. But for Jews every penny is drenched in bitter sweat . . . Dovid, begin Kol Nidre!"

And no sooner had the Holy Baal-Shem spoken those words than the gold rubles in the vestibule of the palace shrank and darkened, while the tiny Jewish coins began shining like glistening stars. And the blind beggar woman's penny was the first to soar up, shred the curtain, and fly to the Throne of Glory. And that penny was followed by all the other Jewish alms.

And in the deserted vestibule of the palace, Satan was left humbled and humiliated.

Repentance

The Jews spent the entire night of Yom Kippur in the synagogue, reciting psalms and not getting a wink of sleep. And all through the night the Jewish Repentance flew up to Heaven and into the vestibule of the palace. There was sighing and moaning, weeping and lamenting, regret and remorse. Confessions flew up from broken hearts, groans from defeated minds, sins and wrongs torn from souls and purged by grief and agony. And all these elements melded into the music of an unearthly song of praise, a song of radiance and righteousness.

When the last spark of Repentance had flown into the vestibule of the palace, Satan the Accuser appeared once again and yelled with icy ferocity: "If the prince's dog brought the Jewish alms to the Throne of Glory, then let that dog testify about Jewish Repentance."

That same instant, the reddish dog, beaten and injured, turned up in the vestibule of the palace, and in front of him stood the prince, hasty and ominous. The trembling dog, fearing another beating, crawled over to the prince's feet, licked his hands, peered slavishly into his eyes, and emitted a woeful yammering.

Satan then grabbed the dog's yammering and trembling and his slavish looks and hurled them over at the Jewish Repentance: "Doesn't the dog's suffering come from the same source as the Jewish Repentance? Shouldn't the angels carry the dog's sighs and his submissive looks to the Throne of Glory together with the human moaning and groaning? After all, they do have the same value . . ."

At the first glints of dawn, with the first weaving of the threads of God's goodness, Volf Kitses came up to the lectern to recite *Shakhres* (morning prayers). But before he could even begin, the Holy Baal-Shem, pulling his tallis (prayer shawl) from his face, turned to the worshipers and asked: "Why did a Jew fast on the tenth of Ab since it is the Ninth of Ab that commemorates the Destruction of the Temple?"

Seeing that no one responded, he said, "I'd like an answer. Why did a Jew fast on the tenth of Ab?"

Since no one replied, he said, "Please answer me: Why did a Jew fast on the tenth of Ab?"

The worshipers merely exchanged glances for no one knew what to say.

The Baal-Shem left his place and headed toward the door, where the poor and the wretched were standing. He walked up to an old pauper, put his hand on his shoulder, and said, "Did you hear my question? Please tell me: Why did a Jew fast on the tenth of Ab?"

The old pauper turned his face from the wall to the Baal-Shem, gaped at him in amazement, and sternly said, "I have nothing to tell and there's nothing I can say . . ."

"But I *need* you to tell me!" the Baal-Shem dug in his heels.

"If *you* need it, then *you* tell us! I don't want to!" the pauper obstinately retorted and turned back to the wall.

The Baal-Shem grinned and, facing the crowd, he said, "Now listen to this story, all of you. No one is to miss a single word of what I'm about to tell you."

The synagogue was filled with a deathly hush, and all eyes were riveted on the Baal-Shem, who now began:

The Baal-Shem's Story

This past Ninth of Ab, an old Jewish pauper came to a small village. Worn out with fasting and with trudging in the heat, he wanted to rest at a Jewish tavern. The innkeeper wasn't at home, and his wife was at the oven, taking out baked rolls and placing them on a board to cool off. Upon seeing the pauper, she went into the next room, brought back a kopeck and gave it to him. The pauper thanked her, and, after relaxing a little, started out again.

A short time later, the woman noticed that one roll was missing. She didn't realize that she had accidentally knocked it to the floor, where it had tumbled underneath the oven. The woman instantly suspected the pauper of stealing the roll. When her husband returned, she told him about the theft. The innkeeper hit the roof.

He then went after the pauper and caught up with him before he reached the next village. He began cursing him for stealing the roll and demanded its return. The pauper swore that he hadn't stolen it. The innkeeper searched him, but, not finding the roll, he furiously screamed: "It's bad enough you're a thief, but you actually ate the stolen roll on a fast day—the Ninth of Ab!" And he beat the pauper within an inch of his life.

For a long time the beaten, bloody Jew lay sprawled out on the road. By the time he regained consciousness, it was already dusk. After reciting Minha (the afternoon prayer), he dragged himself to the next village, where he again stepped into a tavern. The innkeeper suggested that he eat something to end the fast, but he refused. And without a break he fasted one more day—on the tenth of Ab . . .

The Baal-Shem again looked at the crowd in the shul and asked: "Have you listened carefully to my story?"

Now the old pauper turned to the Baal-Shem and shouted angrily: "What do you want from me? What else could I do? A great sin was committed. A Jew suspected an innocent Jew of theft and raised his hand to him. However, the innkeeper didn't realize he was sinning, he actually thought he was doing a mitzvah, a good deed, by punishing a thief and sinner. And since he didn't know he had sinned, he couldn't repent. *I* knew about his sin, though. How could I help but repent for him? So I fasted on the tenth of Ab and I prayed to the

Almighty, asking him to forgive the innkeeper for his innocent sin . . ."

"If that's the case" the Baal-Shem cheerily cried out, "then why is Volf Kitses holding his tongue? C'mon, it's time to recite *Shakhres*!"

And the instant the old pauper finished speaking, all the Jewish repentance started shining as before, and, like a pleasant fragrance, it wafted over to the Throne of Glory.

And Satan, powerless in his wild rage, remained alone in the vestibule of the palace, rejected and humiliated.

Prayer

The Holy Baal-Shem was praying. He was all ablaze with joy and ecstasy. And the words of his prayers, powerful and sparkling, burning in their sweetness, mild and passionate, soared aloft like streaks of flaming diamonds. And they were followed by the prayers of the other worshipers. All through the day, Jewish prayers from the four corners of the world kept rising toward the vestibule of the palace.

The children of Israel were praying. Words resounded, gray and fearful, such as no other language on earth has ever created. There were laments for thousands of years of suffering such as no other nation on earth has ever endured. There were hymns thundering up from a nation that was proud of being chosen, certain of being immortal. There were words that were leviathans, words that encompassed all living things, all created things, from a grain of sand to the most distant planets. There was a wondrous wreath of the softest and humblest acknowledgment of the boundaries of the human mind, the worthlessness of human life, which passes like a fleeting shadow, a melting cloudlet, an illusory dream, and all these things were interwoven with the tender, motherly comforts for the saddened and lamenting Almighty and Eternal.

When the final prayer had faded, when it was time to conclude Yom Kippur by reciting Ne'ilah and time to close the gates of the greatest temple, Satan appeared once again in the vestibule of the palace. Calm in his dark resolve, he began his cruel indictment, using words as sharp as steel blades: "I have come to accuse thieves who have stolen words. All the prayers that are floating here were created by ancient generations, and words that were born in one person's heart cannot form a prayer on another's lips. Is that why the Creator provided human beings with a brain and a mind? Are they supposed to address their Ruler by repeating dead echoes, words that have been rigidified for a thousand years? Doesn't the Good Lord resent accepting as living prayers these ancient words from dead lips—words rubbed smooth like a coin that has been circulating for a thousand years? I demand that the Throne of Glory should admit only those prayers that are recited in strictest observance of all the laws and customs. Prayers should be rejected as defective and unworthy if they omit even a single word, contain even a single mistake; if they are not recited with utmost fervor; if they are interrupted by a side remark, a stray thought, an unnecessary movement; if the prayer shawl slips ever so slightly from the shoulders or the yarmulke from the head. Out here, in the vestibule, there are only two flawless prayers. They were recited by two great rabbis, each of whom, though, has excommunicated the other. I will allow these two prayers to reach the Throne of Glory and I will reject all the rest as faulty and profane."

Satan fell silent. A dense darkness spread through the vestibule of the palace. And the prayers, which had just been blazing, holy and lustrous, now waned and faded, and, as heavy as corpses, they began to sink into the murk. However, the prayers of the two great rabbis blazed in nasty flames, shooting sparks and poison.

And the Gates of Heaven began moving on their hinges and slowly closing: and they would remain shut until the following year.

In a far corner of the shul sat Jacob the innkeeper, who was considered an utter ignoramus even by the other innkeepers. He had an only son, a boy of twelve, who was so obtuse that they couldn't even teach him the alphabet, the alef-beys. Jacob was afraid that if he left him at home all by himself, his son might eat on Yom Kippur. So he took him along and kept him at his side in the shul. All this time, the boy watched hundreds of Jews stretching their arms aloft, lamenting, and praying very ardently. And his mute soul felt an unconscious yearning for prayers and exaltation. But not knowing a single holy word, he had no way of pouring out his sorrows, and so he agonized in silence.

Upon thrusting his hand into his pocket, he found a clay whistle, which he used out in the fields to summon the cattle. He felt like whistling, so he said to his father: "Daddy! I have a whistle on me. I want to blow my whistle!"

The father snapped at him and strictly forbade him to do it. But the boy felt a stronger and stronger desire to whistle, and a short time later he again asked his father to let him do so. The father snapped at him even more sternly and threatened to hit him. But then they began *Mussaf* (the additional prayer recited on the Sabbath and on holidays), and the synagogue was filled with a great outpouring of devotion. Now the boy's craving to whistle grew so intense that he shouted to his father: "Daddy! I can't help myself! I want to blow my whistle!"

The innkeeper felt the boy's whistle through the cloth and crushed it from the outside without interrupting his prayer.

The son felt such passionate yearning to pour out his feelings loudly and strongly that he started shuddering. His torment was so dreadful that he burst into tears.

As a rule the Baal-Shem personally recited Ne'ilah. But when he now stood at the lectern and gazed up at the sky, he trembled at what he saw. He ascended to the Heavens and, upon reaching the palace vestibule, he tried to enter. But the gates were shut, and a heavy padlock hung on them. The Baal-Shem tried to remove the lock, but he couldn't. So he went to the other palaces. But they were filled with such chaos that no one could help him. Then he encountered his Master and he turned to him with a cry: "Rebbe, the Jewish nation is in great danger! Help me to enter the palace vestibule!"

But the Master tearfully replied that he couldn't help him.

So the Baal-Shem went to the prophet Elijah and asked him to open the gates of the palace vestibule. But Elijah replied: "No one has the power to open the gates of the palace except for Jacob, our Patriarch. Go to him!"

So the Holy Baal-Shem went to Paradise. But the sentry angel stood in his way, holding the flaming and flashing two-edged sword that God had placed before the gates of Eden to keep out Adam and Eve. In his great despair, the Baal-Shem shouted in Hebrew: "Jacob! Jacob! Answer me!"

The synagogue quaked with the Baal-Shem's yelling, and Jacob the innkeeper trembled, thinking that the Baal-Shem was calling him. Jacob leaped up, letting go of the crushed whistle, which he had been holding through the cloth.

The instant the boy felt that his pocket was free, he pulled out the whistle, set it to his lips, and emitted a long, loud whistle, which expressed the entire ecstasy and holy exertion of his mute soul.

And the boy's whistling cut through all the heavens, stormed into the vestibule of the palace, shoved away Satan the Accuser, ignited the snuffed prayers, and carried them to the Throne of Glory.

And when Jewish Prayer fused with Jewish Repentance and Charity and reached the lowest step of the Throne of Glory, the Almighty held out His gold scepter and drew the thread of His goodness over them and took them to his bosom. And at that same instant, the dreadful Judgment was rescinded and it changed into Grace and Mercy.

The moment the boy's whistle resounded through the synagogue, the Baal-Shem began reciting Ne'ilah to conclude Yom Kippur. Great were the joy and ecstasy of his worship.

When they finished the evening prayer and the Jews left the shul, the sky was pure, and a full moon hovered in the air. The Holy Baal-Shem blessed the full moon and exuberantly told the worshipers thronging around him: "I hope that God will answer our prayers for a good year, a tranquil and happy year, and that He will not allow a single drop of Jewish blood to be spilled!"

And the crowd replied: "Amen!"

The Girls' Melody

(Folktale)

Years and years ago, when the Ukraine was still a feudal land, and the peasants were the serfs of the aristocracy, the town of Nemirov was ruled by a brutal, wicked, murderous duke. For the sheer pleasure of it, he would whip, thrash, and flog his peasants within an inch of their lives, and he would hang or shoot them for the most trivial crimes. He also constantly persecuted the Jews of Nemirov, virtually bathing in their blood.

One day, the cruel duke decreed that on his birthday the Jews were to bring him the three most beautiful Jewish girls in Nemirov—girls who had not yet known a man.

The Jews were horrified by this dreadful edict. They prayed, they fasted, but none of them could hit on any solution for getting the duke to nullify his decree. So when the scheduled day came, they cast lots, and, amid weeping and lamenting, the three girls designated for this terrible fate were carried off to the duke's palace.

The duke and his guests, who had been boozing and guzzling, were in high spirits when he ordered his servants to bring in the three Jewish girls—stark naked. The instant the girls crossed the threshold, one of them began crooning a sad and poignant melody. Her voice pierced all hearts. The duke and his drunken guests sat there spellbound, absorbed in this extraordinary singing—a kind they had never heard before. And when the girl finished her melody, the noblemen applauded for a long time. They gave the girls expensive presents, did not lay a finger on them, and sent them back to their homes with great pomp and fanfare.

The Jews of Nemirov were ecstatic and they thanked God for this miracle. They quickly learned the melody, which they dubbed "The Girls' Melody," and from then on they joyfully sang it at every religious festivity.

Joy

Dovid-Ber Horovitz

(1923)

Before you, my dear reader, commit a sin and waste a lot of valuable time reading some foolish and trivial story that is utterly impractical and unprofitable, let me tell you a wondrous tale about the Holy Baal-Shem-Tov. It will provide not only great pleasure but also a moral, teaching you all about virtues and good deeds. In the end, I hope, you will turn your steps toward serving God, so that there will be no limit to your rewards.

One summer, Rabbi Israel, the Baal-Shem-Tov (of blessed memory), was with his wife, the virtuous Khana, the daughter of Avrom Mekutev. They were visiting one of his devoted followers, Aaron-Lib Horovitz, a farmer in the village of Yasyen. This Aaron-Lib was renowned for his worldly riches as well as his profound knowledge of the holy texts. For these blessings he thanked the Good Lord not only with prayers but also with good deeds. Thus, he had donated a lovely little shul (synagogue), the only one in the area, plus a bathhouse for the winter. Indeed, people are still talking about them even now.

On holidays the Jews from the surrounding villages would come to pray in the shul. The visitors stayed either in the large rooms of Aaron-Lib's radiant mansion or with the other householders in the village. These local Jews earned their living partly as lumber dealers but chiefly through manual labor: they would drive the timber rafts down the Lumnitsa, then along the mighty Dnyester to Helitsh and sometimes all the way to Odessa . . .

The Jews in this region are big, burly men with very broad shoulders—like Christian peasants (if you'll pardon the comparison). The Baal-Shem greatly enjoyed their company, and they in turn were utterly devoted to him. Supposedly, the Rabbi of Kalish (may he rest in peace) once made fun of them, which terribly annoyed the Baal-Shem, who retorted: "If only all peasants were like mine with their pure, dear, simple hearts!"

And so the Baal-Shem was very pleased to accept his follower's invitation to spend the summer in his home. However, he did not change his normal conduct in any way. He spent his nights at the shul, engrossed in the vast secrets of the Cabala, and his days in the surrounding forests and on the nearby mountains, where all sorts of sheep and cattle were grazing to their hearts' content. Here too, the Baal-Shem could meditate in isolation, indulging in his sublime and holy thoughts. He blessed the beautiful world and he thanked the Good Lord and praised Him for all his gifts.

That region is infinitely beautiful. So at the crack of dawn, right after *Shakhres* (the morning prayer), the Baal-Shem would leave the village and wander across the open fields, where countless blades of grass crooned praises and paeans to their Holy Creator. And how deeply the Baal-Shem understood that wonderful caroling! "With no ulterior motive, no evil thought, and no hope for any reward!" He luxuriated in the fragrance of the surrounding pine forests, their density filled with the endless singing of birds. And he delighted in the chant of the crystal-clear Lumnitsa River, which gushed and surged in its broad, rocky passage through the woods.

Yet he would often recall that of the Ten Divine Attributes of Beauty nine had been granted to the Christians in this area and only one to the rest of the world. And of that one Attribute, only a very tiny sliver had been left to the Children of Israel! To make up for it, the Jews had nine measures of

Wisdom while the rest of the world had only one. But, dear God, what is Wisdom without Beauty?

And the Baal-Shem envied the free nations of the world.

Now on the day of the summer solstice, the Holy Baal-Shem-Tov, meditating, lost in his deep thoughts, strayed too far into the mountains. The day was hot, and the Baal-Shem was thirsty and hungry. But no water was to be found. He had taken some food along, but how could he eat without the ritual of washing his hands? Searching and searching for a well-spring, he grew wearier and thirstier. Meanwhile it was getting late, the sun was already setting. Cooler twilight breezes began to blow. The Baal-Shem started off in the direction of the village, where small, bright windows were cheerily glowing. By now it was already evening, and the village was a long way off!

As he walked along, he suddenly caught the sound of human voices. Healthy rustic lungs were bawling lively and merry ditties into the surrounding mountains, winding each one up with an exultant shout: "HUHAHEY!!!" It was accompanied by a woman's light and lilting, "Huhahey!" and the echo kept responding: "Hey! Hey! Hey!"

The Baal-Shem, overwhelmed with his love of humanity was thrilled to find people in the surrounding hush—and he was also looking forward to eating after washing his hands and saying the benediction over the bread. So he doubled his pace across the soft grass.

Upon drawing closer, he spotted a hut and next to it a stack of dry evergreen logs burning cheerfully and shooting off a spray of lively sparks.

In the light cast by the flames, the Baal-Shem saw a young peasant enjoying himself with a young, partly clad woman. They were having simple, carefree fun—the kind that peasants have. The Baal-Shem was amazed by this sudden and unexpected sight. The two young people were like the lord and lady of the forest with their wild reveling and carousing in this passionate midsummer night. And they emanated the hot smell of bliss and rapture. The smell of youth and life and love . . . Only the smell of sin was missing!

Here, in the healthy mountain air, amid the delightful fragrance of the pine trees, the Baal-Shem fully understood the young couple. He thought to himself: "I can see that God approves of you young people and sanctifies you, and so how can I, a mere mortal, withhold my blessing? . . . Didn't our sages (may they rest in peace) say: 'If the Shekhina (the Divine Manifestation) does not shine in sadness, then how can there be any sin in joy? . . . ' "

And the Baal-Shem blessed them.

Even though he was looking forward so happily to the refreshing water, he did not disturb the lovers. Instead he quickly stole off along the nearby forest trail.

After walking a bit, the Baal-Shem suddenly saw a white, effulgent figure standing on the path and holding a radiant crystal pitcher iridescent with all the splendid colors of the rainbow. He recognized the figure as a messenger from the Celestial Court and, halting in great awe and reverence, he bowed deeply.

"Israel, Israel," the angel cried. "We looked down at you from above and we heard the lament of your starving innards. We felt your steps and we saw that you overcame the Evil Spirit of the Seven Names and that you did not disturb two earthly beings amid their greatest physical joy in the lower world. You profoundly understood the will of God. And so here I, the Angel of Dew, bring you your reward. Today, for your sake, I was dispatched earlier than usual with the sacred pitcher, from which the Good Lord made the first benediction on wine during the Sabbath after the Creation of the Universe. This pitcher is filled with living dew—so drink, Israel!"

The Baal-Shem-Tov made a blessing and he drank and drank . . . And after removing his lips from the pitcher he felt a young, fresh, powerful strength in all the 248 parts of his body. His mind was tremendously clear and sharp, and he believed he could grasp all the mysteries of life. He felt that all previously hidden things would now be revealed to him. Oh, with what ardor, with what ecstasy he would turn the pages of the Zohar, meditating all alone in his little shul . . .

But the Angel of Dew, God's messenger, read the Baal-Shem's mind like an open book, and he said to him: "No,

Israel, tonight you will not study a holy text. You will go home. Khana, your pious and virtuous wife, is tenderly yearning for you. She has been thinking back to her wedding night because today is your anniversary, and for a woman this is a great holiday . . ."

And the Angel of Dew accompanied the Baal-Shem to his home. The road was very radiant, partly because of the huge silvery moon floating across the dark-blue sky and its billions of stars and constellations. But the even greater source of light was the angel's luminous face.

In short, my dear reader, I have no wish to be long-winded. You see, Khana, whose womb had been shut for a long time, had been praying and praying for children. Then, nine months after that night, she gave birth to a daughter, whom they named Hodel. And that baby was the grandmother of the great Chasidic rabbi and storyteller, Nakhman of Braslev (may he rest in peace).

Now you, my pious and zealous reader, are sure to ask: Why is it that the Good Lord did not delight his dearest servant with the son that he so greatly desired—since the eldest son is the one who recites Kaddish, the prayer for the dead, when the parents are buried? Let me explain.

It was Satan's doing. Satan said evil things to the pregnant woman. He insolently disguised himself as a midwife and convinced the pious Khana that she should flout the law and ask God for a daughter without telling her husband. Khana prayed, and her prayers were answered . . .

And do you know why the Devil did that? Because God determined that the firstborn son of the Baal-Shem-Tov was to be endowed with the soul of the Messiah. But, alas, in view of our many sins, the mother herself destroyed this possibility.

So may our Salvation then come from some other source, and may it come soon. Amen.

The Egyptian Passover

S. Ansky

(1920)

Many years ago, while traveling through Egypt, I happened to find myself in Goshen. There, in an antiquities shop, I paid next to nothing for an old, rotting papyrus with nearly faded cuneiform writing. I couldn't read it, but I realized that the manuscript was very ancient and very valuable.

Upon returning to Europe I showed my purchase to a friend of mine, a renowned Egyptologist. No sooner had he taken a look then he joyfully leaped up and exclaimed: "Do you know what a rare find you have here? This document goes back to the era of Ramses the Great! It's about four thousand years old!"

"What does it say?"

"I don't know as yet. I have to go through it sign by sign. But whatever it says, it's an invaluable document—it'll be epoch-making in Egyptological scholarship."

I left the papyrus with him and, understandably impatient, I waited for his response. Within a few days, I received a wire from him: "Hurray! You've unearthed a treasure! The manuscript is a Passover Hagadah, but it's a different version: it's told from the Egyptian instead of the Jewish point of view."

I was very intrigued. The Egyptians were certainly never very pleased with the miracle of Passover—that much was obvious to me. But how did they view all the events? It took my friend several months to decipher the cuneiform script. When he was done, he came to me with the rare document, and we were joined by a Semitologist, who barely spoke throughout the visit.

"The start is missing," said my friend, "and whole sentences are gone from the central portion. But the remaining text gives us a very clear picture of the events of that time. Just listen."

And he began to read: "'A slave from an unknown land, a dangerous dreamer and an interpreter of dreams, very possibly sent by a nearby hostile nation to reconnoiter our country . . .' Here, a lot has faded. But then: ' . . . Imprisoned for a shameful crime against the rich and lofty morals of the noble land of Egypt . . . With glib words [he] stole the heart of divine Pharaoh . . . Seized power . . . Bought up all the grain . . . Became the food dictator . . . Brought in his entire family from Canaan, grabbed Goshen, the best province . . . They were fruitful and multiplied . . . Became masters of the land . . . The whole of Egypt groaned under the burden of their yoke . . .'"

"Another long stretch is missing here. But then it goes on: 'In order to accustom the Jews to productive work, they were given the task of building Pithom and Raamses . . . Were too lazy to work . . . Forced labor had to be introduced . . . Bore terribly many children . . . [We] had to get rid of all infant males, but let the females live . . . Great duplicity in avoiding the laws about getting rid of male children . . . Divine and mild Pharaoh did not mistreat the filthy Jews, He allowed His sacred body to be washed with their blood . . .' And then: 'A yid named Moses appeared . . . Made demands . . . Spoke with unbelievable chutzpah . . . Pharaoh rejected the demands and punished the rebels . . .'

"A lot more is missing here. Then: 'Unhappy Egypt! That criminal Moses used magic to inflict the worst plagues and misfortunes on the land, blood and filth, darkness and epidemics . . . Instead of suppressing the revolutionary movement by sword, Pharaoh, with His usual grace, gave in and permitted the rebels to go and bow to their own god . . . But the wrath of the Almighty God Apis, the Sacred Ox, blazed up and he punished Egypt . . . Instead of being thankful, the departing Jews ignobly robbed the Egyptians of gold and silver . . . The Egyptians pursued the thieves . . . The great catastrophe happened. Yelling and performing their swindling tricks, they stirred up the Red Sea, and it devoured the entire Egyptian army with its horses and chariots . . .'

"The Egyptian Hagadah ends with these words: 'In this way, a vile nation destroyed the great and wealthy land of Egypt, which was world-famous for its huge and strong horses! May the Almighty Apis wreak vengeance on that nation of rebels and tricksters and wipe them from the face of the earth.'"

After finishing the Hagadah, we sat for a while, lost in thought.

"How do you feel about it?" the Egyptologist broke the silence. "I think it's basically correct."

"Correct in what way?" I asked.

"In every way. Egypt was truly a powerful nation. It had the greatest horses. And who destroyed it if not the Jews?"

"Now wait a minute!" I exclaimed. "Let's try and analyze the situation. Listen, as a specialist, an Egyptologist, you must know: Were there any Jews in Egypt before Joseph?"

The Egyptologist pondered a while, then said confidently: "No!"

"So then Joseph was the first Jew to come to Egypt. You won't deny, will you, that he didn't come voluntarily, he was sold into slavery against his will?"

"Granted!"

"Furthermore, Joseph was a dreamer. A dangerous dreamer—*that* I agree with."

"And a profiteer!" the Egyptologist broke in.

"Granted, a profiteer! But tell me: Who forced the Egyptians to make him their lord and master? Even his own brothers didn't much care for his dreams, so they eliminated him. They did so in a barbaric way—but they did get rid of him. And what did the Egyptians do? They sought out his dreams. They ran to consult him in prison and asked him to interpret their dreams. So he gave them the proper explanations. It served them right, the fools!"

"Well, and what about Goshen? After all, Jews did take over the most fertile area of Egypt. Wasn't that immoral of them?"

"Well, wasn't Goshen Goshen before Joseph brought down his family?" I exclaimed. "Why didn't the Egyptians get hold of that region? We may conclude that the Jews didn't *take over* a fertile land—they *made* Goshen fertile. The Egyptians should have been grateful to them."

Both of us fell silent for a time.

"I hope," I then said, "that despite your loyalty, you will nevertheless not judge the Jews all too severely for trying to circumvent and even violate the law ordering them to throw their male babies into the river?"

"Needless to say, it's difficult to blame them for that. That law was truly a wee bit harsh. Though I do feel that no matter how harsh a law, the citizens have to abide by it fully. But let it be. The chief guilt of the Jews in regard to Egypt was the plagues. Think about it. They'd been living in that country for generations, eating their bread there for four centuries, and when Pharaoh wasn't all that quick about giving in to their demand for—let's call it—'national autonomy' or 'minority rights,' they inflicted the worst plagues on that nation! Well, isn't that a crime?"

"Listen to what I have to say!" I exclaimed agitatedly. "I'd never have dreamt you'd believe that stupid libel that it was the Jews who inflicted the plagues on Pharaoh and his country! As a scholar, you ought to know that plagues, especially blood and leprosy, vermin and darkness, can't be inflicted on a nation from the outside. They're caused by domestic factors. A nation develops plagues like this gradually and by itself. If Moses played any part here, it was by way of warning Pharaoh."

"Maybe you're right," the Egyptologist reluctantly conceded. Only then he caught himself: "But the robbery! The theft of gold and silver! You have to admit: a nation is given autonomy, and they start 'cleaning out Egypt'! Why, it's horrible!"

"I won't deny," I replied, "that I'm not too crazy about the way Jews took out 'long-term loans' in Egypt. But what can you expect of slaves? Just think about it. Didn't the Jews basically have a right to take the bit of gold that they got out of Egypt? They'd suffered four hundred years of hard labor, building Pithom and Raamses. Moreover, when they departed, they abandoned all kinds of property—houses, meadows, vineyards. No matter how enslaved the Jews were, a few of them had become millionaires, with villas and palaces. They had to leave all that stuff behind. And how much could the Jews borrow from the Egyptians?! Also, don't forget that back then gold and silver weren't such valuable commodities. The currency exchange rate in Egypt was very high."

The Egyptologist remained silent for a while.

Finally I said: "I assume you won't support the final argument—namely, that the Jews were to blame for the destruction of the Egyptian army and its chariots . . ."

"You're wrong!" the Egyptologist heatedly cried out. "I feel that this very accusation is the most serious and most important one!"

"How is that possible?" I exclaimed. "Why was it the fault of the Jews that the Egyptians threw themselves into the sea?

"It *was* their fault!" He dug in his heels. "Granted, the indictment won't stand up legally. But in moral terms the fault lies entirely with the Jews!"

"In what way?"

"It's quite simple. During those four centuries, the Jews brought a dreamlike mood into Egypt. The Egyptians gradually became accustomed to viewing Jewish dreams as concrete realities. A Jew was a dreamer, but he also knew the meaning of his dreams. The Egyptians were now convinced that 'A Jew knows what he's doing.' And that was what killed the Egyptians! When they chased after the Jews, they had absolutely no intention of diving into the raging waters. But when they saw the Jews hurrying into the sea, they emulated them: 'Hey! If a Jew is jumping in, then there's probably no danger! A Jew knows what he's doing!' And the Egyptians rode into the sea. So wasn't that the fault of the Jews?"

"For God's sake!" I shouted. "I don't understand how you can blame Jews if the Egyptians behaved like jackasses!"

"You don't understand, but I *do*!" he obstinately retorted.

All this time the Semitologist had been listening closely to our conversation without putting in his two kopecks. Now he suddenly exclaimed: "I don't know who can blame whom for more—the Jews the Egyptians or the Egyptians the Jews. Still, there's one thing I'm sure of. No matter how long the Jews may argue, they will never convince the Egyptians that anyone but the Jews is to blame for the destruction of Egypt. Moses already understood that back then . . ."

"Who? Moses our Teacher?" I was flabbergasted.

"The very same! Remember what he said?" And the Semitologist quoted the words in Hebrew [Exodus 14:13]: "'The Egypt that ye have seen today, ye shall see it again no more forever.' Moses accurately prophesied that the plagues, wonders, and miracles would create such a negative attitude toward the Jews that they would never again be able to look at Egypt . . ."

After musing a while, he added: "I'm certain that the Egyptians might have forgiven the Jews for the plagues, the borrowed gold and silver, and even the demolished army. But the horses! The huge, world-famous horses that drew Pharaoh's chariots—for that the worshipers of Apis, the Sacred Ox, will never forgive the Jews!"

During our conversation, the Egyptologist and I had constantly been pointing at the manuscript, fingering a passage here, a paragraph there. We were so engrossed in our debate that we didn't realize we were tearing and tattering the rotten papyrus. By the time we noticed, it was too late—not a trace was left of that rare document from the era of Ramses the Great!

The damage was fearful! But the important thing is that we now know for certain how the Egyptians viewed our Exodus and what they thought about us altogether.

The Rabbi's Melody or A Melody That Unlocks the Secrets of the Torah

(Folktale)

❦

Chasidic Jews have always believed that a melody imbued with the utmost devotion can often shed light on the deep mysteries of the Torah, and to illustrate this they have handed down a story about Rabbi Shnéyer-Zálmen of Lyadi. This rabbi, who also penned several renowned works, was the founder of the Chasidic sect known as Khabad—an acronym for the Hebrew words *Khokhmah* (Wisdom), *Binah* (Intelligence), and *Daas* (Knowledge). Supposedly, whenever he sat down to study the holy texts, he would first sing this Yiddish song with its Hebrew refrain:

The angels and the seraphim,
They all keep asking: "Who is God?"
Alas! What should we answer them?
No mind, no thought can fathom Him,
No mind, no thought can fathom Him,
No mind, no thought can fathom Him.

The nations all around the earth
They all keep asking: "Where is God?"
Alas! What should we answer them?
There is no place where He is not,
There is no place where He is not,
There is no place where He is not.

According to tradition, Rabbi Shnéyer-Zálmen composed ten melodies for the ten Sephirot, the mystical Spheres of the universe. One of these melodies, which became very popular among Chasidim, is called "The Rabbi's Melody." In regard to this melody, which is sung even today in all the Jewish communities, the following tale has come down to us.

During a Sabbath meal, Rabbi Shnéyer-Zálmen was explaining a holy text to his disciples. While speaking, he noticed an unfamiliar elderly Jew sitting across from him at the table. The rabbi had never seen him before. The stranger, all ears and focusing entirely on the rabbi, hung on his every word. But though he was doing his best to understand the teachings, he was unable to fathom anything, and a deep sorrow spread across his face.

Afterwards, when the rabbi went into his private study, he sent for the stranger and asked him whether he had gleaned anything from today's lesson. The man burst out crying and, with a heavy heart, he admitted that he had grasped nothing of the holy words. With tears in his eyes, he explained that he had lost his father at a very early age and that his mother had been too poor to keep him in school. The boy had had no choice but to help her and so he had gone to work. Somewhat later he had married, so that supporting his wife and then their children had left him no time for study. He had been limited to reciting the psalms, but he didn't even fully understood the Psalter that he recited every day. Now that he was old, and his children were all married, he felt a powerful urge to study the Torah, but the scholars at the synagogue laughed at him.

"Rabbi, I've heard that you befriend all people, and so I've come to you and I've sat down at your table just like all the others. You have no idea how happy I was to be treated as an equal among equals! But when you began speaking, and I saw that I was completely lost, I felt awful, and my joy disappeared. Rabbi! Holy Rabbi! What should I do to be worthy of becoming your student and understanding your teachings?"

With his head hanging, and tears streaming into his beard, the man fell silent. The rabbi then put his right arm around him and said in a soft voice: "Stop crying! This is the Sabbath, and no one should be sad on the Sabbath! Today I explained the teachings of the Baal-Shem-Tov. And if you didn't understand me through words, then you will understand through music. I will now sing a melody that contains all the beliefs of the Baal-Shem-Tov."

And Rabbi Shnéyer-Zálmen began crooning the sweetest of melodies, phrase by phrase. The elderly man listened with all his heart and soul. He stood there, transfixed, not batting an eyelash, and as the melody drew on, his face became more and more radiant. He glowed with happiness, and a warm joy poured through all his limbs. When the singing was done, the exuberant and euphoric Jew exclaimed: "Rabbi! I understand! I can see it all! I feel that I'm worthy of being your student!"

From then on, after giving his lesson, Rabbi Shnéyer-Zálmen would always sing that same melody for any listeners who hadn't fully grasped his words. He thereby provided a second explanation through the music, and his piece is known to this day as "The Rabbi's Melody."

S. ANSKY, pseudonym for Shloyme Zanul Rappoport, was a Russian-born writer and folklorist. *The Dybbuk*, Ansky's only complete dramatic work, was written in 1914 and was first produced by the Vilna Troupe in 1920, two weeks after his death.

TONY KUSHNER's plays include *A Bright Room Called Day, Angels in America, A Gay Fantasia on National Themes, Part One: Millennium Approaches* and *Part Two: Perestroika; Slavs!: Thinking About the Longstanding Problems of Virtue and Happiness;* and adaptations of Goethe's *Stella*, Brecht's *The Good Person of Setzuan*, and *The Illusion,* freely adapted from Corneille. For *Angels in America*, Mr. Kushner was awarded the 1993 Pulitzer Prize for Drama, the 1993 and 1994 Tony Award for Best Play, the 1993 and 1994 Drama Desk Award, the 1992 Evening Standard Award, two Olivier Award nominations, the 1993 New York Drama Critics Circle Award, and the 1994 LAMBDA Liberty Award for Drama. His work has been produced at theatres around the United States and in more than thirty countries.

JOACHIM NEUGROSCHEL has translated 160 books from French, German, Italian, Russian and Yiddish, including works by Kafka, Chekhov, Bataille, Sholem Aleichem, and Nobel laureates Thomas Mann, Elias Canetti and Albert Schweitzer. In 1996 he was made a chevalier in France's Ordre des Arts et des Lettres.